PRAISE FOR *A BLAZE IN A DESERT*

"The voice of Victor Serge is need ever, and
James Brook provi f his poems,
bringing out the ssion and
sensibility, and h gement.
History and the cos s, dreams
and loss trace a ving collection."

—Bill Marshall, author of *Victor Serge: The Uses of Dissent*
and *Guy Hocquenghem: Beyond Gay Identity*

"In these dark times, the poetry of Victor Serge illuminates the
deep continuum of revolutionary history. As all great work,
it shows the power of both resistance & acceptance. Serge
is noted for his prose but his poetry is in many ways more
moving. It inspires the reader to stay true to the revolutionary
spirit and will in its compassion, defiance, and outrage."
—David Meltzer, author of *San Francisco Beat: Talking with the
Poets*, *When I Was a Poet*, and *Two-Way Mirror: A Poetry Notebook*

"In this meticulously translated collection of Victor Serge's
poetry, emotion is the force that swells beneath the poet's
acute observations and his reasoning, sobriety, and restraint."
—Summer Brenner, author of *Nearly Nowhere* and *My Life in Clothes*

"An international rebel with a cause, ever the champion
of the downpressed and foreclosed, and of 'all the broken
young wings,' Victor Serge—deported, exiled, hounded from
country to country and continent to continent—inhabited
a 'planet without visas.' But in *A Blaze in a Desert* Serge's
poetry, which witnessed the rise of modern totalitarian
political ideologies and ideologues, comes home to Walt
Whitman's band of brothers. And James Brook's erudite
introduction guides us well through Serge's engagement with
poetry and poets and the enduring struggle for justice."
—Gloria Frym, author of *Mind over Matter* and *The True Patriot*

A Blaze in a Desert

A Blaze in a Desert: Selected Poems
Victor Serge

Translated and edited by James Brook

Afterword by Richard Greeman

A Blaze in a Desert: Selected Poems by Victor Serge
Translation and edition copyright © 2017 by James Brook
Afterword copyright © 2017 by Richard Greeman

This translation is based on Victor Serge, *Pour un brasier dans un désert*, Jean Rière, ed., published in France in 1998. The new translations of *Résistance* and "Mains" in *A Blaze in a Desert* supersede the translations in the 1989 City Lights edition of those poems.

ISBN: 978–1–62963–382–4
Library of Congress Control Number: 2016959587

Cover drawing copyright © 1978 by Vlady
Cover design by John Yates / www.stealworks.com
Interior design by briandesign

10 9 8 7 6 5 4 3 2 1

PM Press
PO Box 23912
Oakland, CA 94623
www.pmpress.org

Printed in the USA by the Employee Owners of Thomson-Shore
in Dexter, Michigan.
www.thomsonshore.com

Contents

II. Messages

III. Mains/Hands

Preface

Many years ago, friends pressed me to read Victor Serge's writings, especially *Memoirs of a Revolutionary* and the novels. These books turned out to be among a handful that preserved and helped recreate the human texture of an era of revolt, revolution, and darkly tragic counterrevolution that still weighs on the present. The writing was vivid, stirring, tense, modern—a source of divided pleasures in "our night with its stars askew."

I came to the poetry much later, stumbling across François Maspéro's 1972 reprint of *Résistance* (retitled *Pour un brasier dans un désert*) in a bookshop in Paris one day. The poems, many of them written during the "immense shipwreck" of Stalin's ascendancy, struck me as strange, oblique, and often beautiful: they were charged with anger, hope, disappointment, irony, and passion, and they quickly shifted from clear-eyed realism to lyricism to the crack-up of the real, and back again.

A Blaze in a Desert includes translations of *Résistance* (1938), Serge's sole published book of poems, and of *Messages* (1946), a manuscript left unpublished until 1998. In addition, it contains a translation of Serge's last poem, "Mains" (Hands) (1947), also left in manuscript. Throughout, I have relied on Jean Rière's superb edition of the poems: Victor Serge, *Pour un brasier dans un désert* (1998); his annotated edition also includes uncollected and unpublished poems and drafts of poems.

I owe a debt of gratitude to Mitchell Abidor, Claudio Albertani, Lori Fagerholm, and Georgia Smith for their encouragement and help over the years that this project took. Special thanks are due to Christopher Winks, Donald Nicholson-Smith, Renée Morel, Richard Greeman, and Summer Brenner for their crucial readings and comments when such were most needed. Richard Greeman, the translator of most of Serge's novels, also contributed the afterword. El Centro Vlady, at the Universidad Nacional Autónoma de México (UNAM), graciously authorized the reproduction of the sketch that Vladimir Kibalchich Russakov (Vlady) made of his father's hands in death.

Lori, this book is for you.

James Brook
November 2016

Mourning the Fallen, Mourning the Revolution

James Brook

> All my life I have seen only troubled times, extreme divisions in society, and immense destruction; I have taken part in these troubles.
> —Guy Debord, *Panegyric*, vol. 1

Victor Serge (1890–1947) is best known for *Memoirs of a Revolutionary* and a series of novels based on his experience of prison in France, a failed insurrection in Spain, the early hopes and abysmal failure of the Russian Revolution, the fall of France to the invading German army, and the epic chaos of the Second World War.[1] But from his anarchist youth in Belgium and France till his dying day in Mexico after the Second World War, Serge was also very much a poet. Elegiac, satiric, sometimes lyrical, his poetry speaks of experiences almost incomprehensible to us, because we are so distant from Serge's world and our sense of history is often so weak. As he asks in his wartime notebooks, "What remains of the worlds I've known, in which I've struggled?"[2] As with his memoirs, one of the tasks of Serge's poetry is to preserve and transmit the memory of those densely populated worlds.

Serge wrote much of his poetry in exile. As a prisoner of Stalin, Serge spent the years 1933–1936 in internal deportation in Orenburg, near the Russian border with Kazakhstan, where he wrote most of the poems published in *Resistance* (1938). Later, in his flight from the Nazi invasion of France, Serge found refuge in Mexico, where he lived from 1941 until his death in 1947. He began writing the poems collected in

Messages (1946) in Paris and Marseille, with others datelined Martinique, Ciudad Trujillo, the Atlantic, and Mexico.[3]

For Serge, exile meant more than geographical displacement. As a core member of the Left Opposition to Stalin from the late 1920s on, Serge lived amid intense ideological conflicts that often put his life in jeopardy. From his early days as an anarchist in Belgium and France, through his participation in the Russian Revolution, and till the end of the Second World War, Serge lived the great hopes and the bitter disappointments of social revolution in the first half of the twentieth century. He witnessed the rise of first Stalinist, then Nazi totalitarianism, and he saw the world utterly transformed by a war in ways that he struggled to comprehend, all of which left their imprint on his poetry, as in "Marseille" (1941):

> Planet without visas, without money, without compass,
>   great empty sky without comets,
> The Son of Man has nowhere left to lay his head,
> His head a target for mechanical shooters,
> His Remington portable and his last suitcase
> Bearing the names of fifteen fallen cities . . .

Serge was a lifelong outsider. As the child of anti-czarist Russian exiles in Belgium, he was born into the bitter estrangement from bourgeois society that would lead him to individualist anarchism and to the intoxications of poetry in vogue in that milieu.[4] Serge was a poet partly due to the curse of self-awareness and his conviction that the world did not have to be impoverished, unjust, and unfree. He was in effect a poète maudit in the tradition of French poets that stretches from Villon to Baudelaire and up through Surrealism. This conscious alienation, so evident in the anarchist writings of the young Serge,[5] evolved to include rebellion against the stifling bureaucratic collectivism of the USSR.

Serge's poetry has roots in the fertile Symbolist soil that nurtured Guillaume Apollinaire's and Émile Verhaeren's poetry, a soil that had been enriched by Walt Whitman's long line and large spirit. Like Apollinaire, Serge can write dense, enigmatic lyrics; like Verhaeren and Whitman,[6] he can enter imaginatively and sympathetically into the lives of others, no matter how different from himself. And like Jehan Rictus, a sort of ventriloquist of poverty, he has an ear for the voices of the down and out. Echoes of Baudelaire and Rimbaud also reverberate in Serge's poetry.[7]

During his time in the Soviet Union, Serge was a familiar of many Russian poets, including Osip Mandelstam and Boris Pasternak. Among the Russian Symbolists, Serge's themes have affinities with Alexander Blok's, as in "The Twelve," an antic poem that highlights irreconcilable conflicts within the Russian Revolution, and "The Scythians," in which the Russian spirit is torn between Europe and Asia. And while Andrei Bely's *Petersburg* is especially important to Serge's evolution as a novelist, Serge seems also to recruit Bely's exclamatory, fractured style in poems like "Mexico: Morning Litany" and "Outbreaks," in which the mad violence of the Second World War is dramatized in sharp-edged fragments.

Serge's novels often incorporate poetry, including his own. In *The Long Dusk*, his novel of the fall of France, Serge creates Félicien Mûrier, a late-Symbolist poet who mentally composes a poem as he wanders through the Chirico cityscape of a Paris whose streets are emptying out as the Wehrmacht advances.[8] The first couplet of Mûrier's poem is from "Song," given here in Ralph Manheim's translation:[9]

> the archer succumbs, the rock splits
> the flower is a cry triumphant—

"Song," which is inspired by Apollinaire's "La Chanson du mal-aimé" (The Song of the Poorly Loved), also figures in *The Case of Comrade Tulayev*: near the end of the novel, Romachkin plucks from the shelf "a book by a poet whose name he did not know" and begins reading where the book falls open, on the last stanza of "Song" (in Willard R. Trask's translation):

Divine revolving planet
thy Eurasias thy singing seas
simple scorn for the headsmen
and behold a merciful thought we are
almost like unto heroes

Romachkin wonders: "But why is there no punctuation? Perhaps because thought, which embraces and connects by invisible threads (but do such threads exist?) planets, seas, continents, headsmen, victims, and ourselves, is ever fluid, never rests, stops only in appearance?"[10] This restless infiltration of poetry into prose fiction disturbs the relationships between fiction, poetry, writer, reader, and reality—because poetry is inherently undermining, destabilizing . . .

Wallace Stevens, the premier American poet in the Symbolist tradition, had long meditated on the relationships between fiction, poetry, writer, reader, and reality. As remote as his work is from Serge's, Stevens brings Serge into canto XIV of "Esthétique du Mal" (1947) and engages him in a kind of dialogue of the deaf about logic, madness, politics, and—ultimately—poetry:

Victor Serge said, "I followed his argument
With the blank uneasiness which one might feel
In the presence of a logical lunatic."
He said it of Konstantinov. Revolution
Is the affair of logical lunatics.[11]

Konstantinov: In the early 1920s, as a member of the Cheka (the political police), Konstantinov had crossed swords with Serge; in the late 1920s, when Serge was in the Left Opposition, Konstantinov confided to him his theory that the Central Committee had long been betrayed from within. He tells Serge that "he knows the names, he has the proofs." Although Serge is repelled by the man and his paranoid delusions, he sees that "in all that [Konstantinov] says, he is driven by one basic idea that is not the idea of a madman: 'We did not create the Revolution to come to this'"[12]—"this" being the New Economic Policy, which unleashed a revitalized private capitalism whose corruption and growing inequality threatened to sweep away the gains, however equivocal, of the revolution. It is Stevens, not Serge, who judges that "Revolution / Is the affair of logical lunatics." In Serge's view, Konstantinov is symptomatic of the failings of a revolution that Serge remains intent on saving, despite everything.

No doubt Stevens would have considered Serge himself as yet another madman. And if Stevens had known of Serge's poetry, perhaps he would have dismissed it as poetry covered by ideological blinders. But Serge was not a Konstantinov or "the lunatic of one idea / In a world of ideas, who would have all the people / Live, work, suffer and die in that idea." If anything, Serge, whose poetry comes to grips with reality's sharp corners, would agree with Stevens that "The greatest poverty is not to live / In a physical world" (canto XV). Another unlikely intersection of the poets: Stevens is also the author of "The Men That Are Falling," in which he interrogates the apparition on his pillow of the bodiless head of a Republican soldier fallen in the Spanish Civil War: "This man loved earth, not heaven, enough to die."[13]

Over the years, Serge continually engaged in a productive quarrel with Surrealism, a late-blooming branch of Symbolism. He had a long and difficult friendship with André Breton, and he knew many other Surrealists in Paris before the war. Later, Breton and Wifredo Lam accompanied Serge and his son Vlady (who was to become a well-known Mexican painter) on the *Capitaine Paul-Lemerle* as they all sailed from Marseille into exile in 1941.[14] Serge and his companion, Laurette Séjourné, collected artwork by their friend Victor Brauner. And in Mexico, Serge's circle included Benjamin Péret, Pierre Mabille, and Leonora Carrington. There, he also became friends with Octavio Paz, to whom he introduced the poetry of Henri Michaux and for whom Serge's dissident Marxism was a decisive influence on his break with Stalinism.[15]

Although Serge was sympathetic to Surrealist painting, he was impatient and critical of Surrealist poetry. The sources of this distaste are obscure; in fact, he seems torn between repulsion and attraction to Surrealist poetry. He was also of two minds regarding Surrealism as a movement: while in a notebook entry Serge approves of the Surrealist movement for its "revolt against the debased reason" of bourgeois common sense and conformism, he is alarmed that it aims at the intellect itself, at "the rational intelligence that built science and philosophy." Surrealist rebellion, in Serge's estimation, is "strictly literary, stuck in Paris cafés and reviews" and "in search of shock effects—scandal, publicity—not revolutionary effects that are useful and liberating," in addition to "aiming only for a select, often rich audience." Nonetheless, Serge continually returns in *Carnets* to his argument with Surrealism and Surrealists, as the many references to Breton, Péret, and others attest. His barbed criticism is often coupled with qualified praise: "The movement can be considered revolutionary for the time being because it leads to taking a stand counter to the reigning conditions (Henri Michaux: 'I counter,' very strong)."[16]

In a rare instance of convergence at the end of the war, Serge and Péret, a Trotskyist militant and a veteran of the Spanish Civil War, published their moral and political critiques of French Resistance poets, including former Surrealists Paul Éluard and Louis Aragon. Both Serge and Péret rebuked such poets for remaining silent about Stalinist tyranny even as they combated Nazi tyranny. Still, while Serge acknowledges the courage of Resistance poets in their perilous situation, Péret will have none of it as he attacks his former Surrealist comrades for their newfound nationalism, their vague religiosity, and their betrayal of the subversive spirit of poetry. Regarding the quality of the poetry, Péret writes: "Not one of these 'poems' surpasses the lyrical level of pharmaceutical advertising."[17]

In a later notebook entry, the argument with Surrealist poetry comes to the fore as Serge struggles with a line from a Péret poem in order to distinguish his own approach to writing:[18]

> The game of Surrealists and aesthetes consists of looking for unexpected comparisons: "The egrets of voice springing from the burning bush of lips" (Benjamin Péret)—that's excellent because it's possibly spontaneous; but I doubt that one can produce many spontaneous (or elaborated) images of this quality without mental concentration on this production, a concentration that must do harm to thought in general, to observation, to other concerns. Rather than inventing unusual or simply new images, I prefer considering things with simplicity, depicting them in ordinary words, and following the course of my problems. And I don't think a middle term exists.

So the literary game called Surrealism can produce "excellent" images—the writing of which may be harmful to the poet. By implication, such images are empty, decorative—whether spontaneous or invented. (In fact, Péret's poetry, which Paz, for one, admired, was known for its effortless spontaneity and for its superabundance of startling images.) And the alternative? Serge seems to propose that the poet should aim for straightforward description via transparent language—that is, a more or less classical style. His criticism of Surrealist poetry can turn even harsher: "From Gongorism to the most insipid ornamental literature, the [Surrealist] line of research has consisted in this: embellish reality, scorn the direct expression of reality."[19]

All the same, Serge is deeply attracted to Péret's line; he may even have memorized it, given that he makes small errors in transcription when he writes "Les aigrettes de voix jaillissant du buisson ardent des lèvres," instead of "Les aigrettes de ta voix jaillissant du buisson ardent de tes lèvres" (The egrets of your voice springing from the burning bush of your lips), as the line appears in Péret's *Je Sublime* (I Sublimate), a book of ecstatic love poetry. Given the intensity of Serge's passion for Séjourné and the difficulties of their relationship, perhaps the forgetting of the possessive adjectives ("*ta* voix" and "*tes* lèvres") tells of unconscious conflicts. Moreover, the choice of text to illustrate his argument seems no more accidental than the errors of memory or transcription. As for Serge's own approach, it is far from Surrealist, but it is surely more complex, ambivalent, and ambiguous than "the direct expression of reality."

If there is a roughly contemporary poet in English who is close to Serge in spirit and in poetics, it is Kenneth Rexroth (1905–1982), who was politically radical, independent of mind, a deeply cultured autodidact, a literary translator (particularly of classical Chinese and Japanese poetry), and a prime instigator of the San Francisco Renaissance following the Second World War. Rexroth and Serge never met, but Rexroth was aware of Serge—and in one poem Serge evokes a presence like Rexroth's during San Francisco's radical heyday in the 1930s. In an uncanny moment in "Frontier" (the first poem in *Resistance*), Serge, "a torn man of Eurasia," looks westward past Europe to "Greater Europe" and to "Frisco where the IWWs live," which is "on the frontier of the next, Greater War," and asks:

> What eyes straining toward Asia peer at the Ocean over
> there,
> eyes sad like mine from sounding this tangible void
> where continents begin and end,
> through the silence of the other human face?

Serge wrote "Frontier" in his city of exile, Orenburg; the poem was published in Paris in September 1934, a few months after the San Francisco General Strike, which Serge possibly had news of. "What eyes straining toward Asia"? Clairvoyance, correspondence, or coincidence provides a purely imaginary, poetic but fitting response: Rexroth, a former Wobbly, was deeply involved with the left and organizing in the city at the time—while butting heads with local Stalinists. Also in this period, Rexroth, turning away from avant-garde poetry, was beginning to write the more direct poems of *In What Hour* (1940), some of which are strikingly similar to Serge's Orenburg poems in language, tone, theme, and imagery. Like Serge, Rexroth can quickly shift from musical and poetic to prosaic and sententious. Take, for example, "Another Early Morning Exercise," with its references to the constellations and its sense of place, persons, and politics in a time of war:[20]

> The moon falls westward in a parabola from Castor
>   and Pollux.
> I walk along the street at three in the morning.
> . . .
> I have been sitting in Sam Wo's drinking cold aromatic
>   liquor.
> "What did Borodin do in Canton in 1927"—
> The argument lasted five hours.
> My friend Soo sympathizes with the Left Opposition;
> . . .
> Whatever Borodin did was probably wrong;
> History would be so much simpler if you could just
>   write it
> Without ever having to let it happen.
> . . .
> A chill comes over me; I walk along shivering;
> Thinking of a world full of miserable lives,
> And all the men who have been tortured
> Because they believed it was possible to be happy.

In his 1963 review of the first English translation of *Memoirs of a Revolutionary* ("What a tale!"), Rexroth mentions writing to Serge in Marseille, and he notes that "Serge was the author of several moving novels, and a man of great humanity and sensitivity."[21] Though Rexroth may have been ignorant of Serge's poetry, he does notice qualities in the memoirs that are also present in the novels and the poetry. Referring to Stalin's murderous purges, for example, Rexroth writes: "We all know the story, but Serge knew the people. They come alive, seen not with Trotsky's epigrammatic malice, but with pity and understanding, and then they die, and Serge feels each death himself. Something in him dies each time." And in their poetry, both Rexroth and Serge mourn the deaths of revolutionaries and revolutions. For Serge especially, many of those closest to him were entered into the register of the names of the lost.[22]

The elegiac mode holds sway in Serge's poetry, especially in *Resistance*: everywhere are elegies to the dead, to "the hope-filled cortege of his executed brothers" ("Sensation"); even poems about the living are often elegiac. In "Constellation of Dead Brothers," for example, Serge names a long series of friends and comrades—including one Nguyen, later known as Ho Chi Minh, whose death had been reported in error—before acknowledging his debt to them and his resolve to continue their fight:

> Oh rain of stars in the darkness,
> constellation of dead brothers!
>
> To you I owe my blackest silence,
> my resolve, my indulgence
> for all these seemingly empty days,
> and whatever is left to me of pride
> for a blaze in a desert.

Against the darkness of the skies, the times, and the mood, the dead are falling stars—fleeting sparks of activity, feeling, and consciousness. But by dint of Serge's commemoration as he writes from his place of exile, they are also the fixed stars that will guide him through life, despite looming fatality, in all senses of the word.

In mourning the living—that is, the not yet dead—"Boat on the Ural" is a counterpoem to "Constellation of Dead Brothers": A group of deported Oppositionists has taken a boat out on the river for the day, and they are very much alive as they row against the current, singing to keep their spirits up. But midway through the poem, an image recalls the deaths of others who "fell / from heaven to a brilliant death"—which echoes the "rain of stars" in "Constellation of Dead Brothers." When the journey to nowhere comes to its end, along with the momentary illusion of freedom on the river ("smiles in the depths of the water, / prison bars on the pale sky"), the penultimate stanza is almost Chinese in its muted anguish:

> Night falls, the boat pulls in,
> stop singing.
> Exile relights its captive lamps
> on the shore of time.

"Death of Panait," one of Serge's major poems, is a testament to his friendship with the Romanian writer Panait Istrati. In many ways a traditional elegy, "Death of Panait" mourns the friend and celebrates his qualities, his pleasures, and his troubles as it indicts his enemies. A meditation on the uncertainties of life and the finality of death, it is also a search for reconciliation amid the grief of an irreparable loss.[23]

Istrati was the author of tales of adventure set in the Balkans that, to Serge, were proof of "an inner lyrical life that is hard to define." Indeed, Serge describes him as "a born poet madly in love with simple things like adventure, friendship, rebellion, flesh and blood."[24] For many years, Istrati had led a rough-and-tumble, vagabond existence before he turned to writing, with Romain Rolland's encouragement; his novels met with immediate success.

In 1927 Istrati was invited to Moscow for the celebration of the tenth anniversary of the October Revolution, where he met the Greek writer Nikos Kazantzakis. Together with their companions, they roamed the country in order to see Soviet life with their own eyes. As an unexpected result, Istrati lost his initial enthusiasm for all things Bolshevik and came away feeling bitterly disappointed by the abuses of power, the corruption, the univocal party line, the suppression of free speech, the atmosphere of fear and intimidation, and the arbitrary detentions that he witnessed. Back in France, Istrati wrote of his disillusionment in *Vers l'autre flamme, après seize mois dans l'U.R.S.S.* (Toward the Other Flame: After Sixteen Months in the USSR).[25] The book earned him intense calumny and vilification at the hands of party hacks and others both in the USSR and in Europe who accused him of betraying the revolution and even of working for the Romanian security services. One of Istrati's unpardonable sins was exposing the intense persecution of Serge's wife, Liuba Russakova, and her family: Serge's father-in-law, Alexander Russakov, a Jewish anarchist worker, had been denounced as "a counterrevolutionary, ex-capitalist, anti-Semite, and terrorist," and the whole family was put in jeopardy.[26] Sick in body and sick at heart, Istrati eventually returned to Romania, where he died of tuberculosis at the age of 50 in 1935.

In the first two-thirds of "Death of Panait," the repetition of the word "finished" rings like a muffled bell as incidents of travail and delight in Istrati's past life are recited. Early stanzas recall Istrati's taking leave of women and of the seductions of wandering—that is, of two of his most enduring passions outside of writing:

> Finished—the romances, dark lips and golden eyes
> in the back of some dive, in the ports,
> in the depths of the night.

> Finished—the bitter,
> intoxicating
> temptations of the sea.

As Istrati is progressively despoiled by death, the poem comments on his choice of friends in life, which prompts him to take a swipe at the unreliability of writers:

> But maybe they were good men,
> and maybe they were saints,
> your pals
> in the little café in Brăila
> where tough customers
> smuggled contraband
> at the Paradise.

> "Not one, you see, not one of them
> would've left the other in the lurch.
> They weren't writers."

Serge, himself the target of even worse mistreatment, knew how Istrati suffered from the abuse received at the hands—or pens and typewriters—of "all those phrasemongers" who called him "a sellout":

> You lay upon your press clippings, like Job upon his filth,
> gently spitting up the last remnant of your lungs
> into the faces of the hacks,
> the glorifiers of profitable massacres,
> the profiteers of disfigured revolutions . . .

> Finished—even the wish to die
> when only bastards are left in this vale of promotional
>   tears.

His torments almost at an end, Istrati is helped along "the road's burning stones" toward death in all its finality—"the sky is blinding, ah, what heartbreak!"—by "two goddesses" who are called "solitude, friendship." Life may have finished with Istrati, but Serge has not finished mourning his friend:

> No more will I see you going from room to room

stirring your black mood
into your cup of black coffee.
No more will I calm your vehement rages.
No more will I see your veiny Balkan hands,
your big, gold-filled mouth,
your hunter's nose, your eyes of a sly old child,
a cynic among the cunning . . .

In the French original of "Death of Panait," the exclamation "what heartbreak!" is "quel déchirement!" Among the key words in Serge's poetry are the noun *déchirement*, the adjectives *déchiré* and *déchirant*, and the verbs *déchirer* and *se déchirer*. The semantic field includes tearing, ripping, rending, splitting, with literal and figurative senses that depend on the context. When in the last line of "Frontier" Serge describes himself as "a torn man of Eurasia," the French is "un homme déchiré d'Eurasie." In "People of the Ural," a young woman is singing when "her voice turns gently heartrending"—"la voix devient doucement déchirante." And in "Mexico: Churches," the sense of *déchirer* combines the concrete and the figurative in "a heavy cloud . . . tearing open . . . the Milky Way."

The *déchirement* series, however rendered in English, opens a way into the poetry of a torn man, for Serge's life can be viewed as a set of conflicting, seemingly irreconcilable pairs, such as anarchism and Bolshevism, individualism and collectivism, literature and action, vulnerability and toughness, sanity and madness, power and powerlessness, and Europe and Asia (with eventually a third term, Mexico).[27] But as important as the *déchirement* series may be, it is only one of Serge's resources in conveying his sense of inner and outer conflicts: Imagery is another, including images of torture and crucifixion. And so are the broken forms of whole poems that mimic the broken world they present; for in these poems, when things fall apart, so do their representations.

"Outbreaks," for example, is flooded by a whirl of images related to high-altitude bombing (an innovation of the Second World War), in which an "angel-faced aviator" destroys the planet as he just follows orders, "for his head was equipped with brand-new ideas made of a metal that was superflex-ible, durable, unbreakable, and cheap." The immediate result: "the planet split into . . . six hundred and sixty-six parts, / six hundred and sixty-six decapitated little girls under the rubble" of a school. Enter Alfred Jarry's Père Ubu, who, thrown into a rage because his collections of chamber pots and postage stamps were destroyed, threatens "a nice little revolution with mass-produced guillotines, standardized, electrified, et cetera / and statues of jerks in uniform on every street corner, you'll see!" The physical world, as well as the social world, is shat-tered, and poetry cannot put it back together again.

A longing for refuge and relief from unending struggle, suf-fering, and tension appears in many poems, evidence of a deep-seated wish for an "anywhere out of this world." Yet a particular image of calm does eventually emerge from the agony of two poems, "Tête-à-Tête" and "Song," an image that conjures up a Baudelairean idyll or Watteau's *The Embarkation for Cythera*—transposed of course to very different circum-stances. In "Tête-à-Tête," a poem that discloses the hard trials of Liuba's mental illness, Serge sketches a definition of "that great word *peace*":

> slack waves at dawn under new leaves,
> innocent leaves,
> a welcome, a presence, a fulfillment,
> there is what is not, what will *never* be.

"Song" is more cryptic and condensed in its troubledness as it envisions a similar island of repose: "Imagine if you found peace again / that slack water beneath the palms." But in an irony of personal history, as Serge sailed to exile in Mexico he discovered the Caribbean to be a "voracious sea, [a] dangerous sea" that sings a "menacing song." Serge experienced the islands as hellish sites of conquest, slavery, and genocide, and the sea as sinister: "The surge of your low waves toward these lush lands is like a surge of hatred, / The palm trees . . . are shredded by it" ("Caribbean Sea"). Even earlier, in part III of "Dialectic," he had compared "the wild and sinister / sound of waves" to "the sound of a crowd" and to the "muffled sound" of "throat-slitting."

In "Mexico: Churches," Serge attempts a deeper resolution—a reconciliation—of the conflicts that tear him and the world apart. To this end, he uses a kind of hallucinatory juxtaposition to unite places distant in time and in space: Russia and Mexico, places that are important to his grappling with life in the wake of a failed revolution and a new world war. Perhaps surprisingly for an atheist revolutionary, the emblematic sites are churches: "the flamboyant crimson church of Pushkino" in Russia and a church in San Juan Parangaricutiro near the newly formed Paricutín volcano in Mexico:[28]

> The two most Christian churches I have seen combine
> in my memory
> thus two rising flames join one crimson and the other
> black
> thus continental expanses merge the tropics and
> suddenly the pole
> the jungle and suddenly the steel of glaciers
> inseparable in their inexplicable unity

The images of the churches combine in the poet's memory, granted, but here Serge risks playing down the element of poetic imagination, which energizes and dramatizes this connection, a connection that the poem itself enables. Is Rimbaud *le voyant* so far away when writing in *A Season in Hell*, "I grew accustomed to simple hallucination: I quite simply saw a mosque in place of a factory . . . a salon at the bottom of the lake"? The irrational joining of disparate but juxtaposed realities, with each carrying its own specific affective charge, is not so much a technique as a product of the imagination at work. Rimbaud also haunts the description of the youthful Serge at the church in Pushkino:

> and we were reconciled with the cold with the northern
> lights
> with the polar nights
> with the convulsive nights and the obsessive suns that
> each carried in his head
> (We were young travelers joyfully bitter and strong on
> intimate terms with torments and death
> we had real need of reconciliation with ourselves and
> the work of human hands)

Even so, the main thrust of "Mexico: Churches" implicitly contradicts Rimbaud, whose watchword was refusal, not reconciliation, and who vociferously denounced the work of human hands: "I detest all occupations . . . What a century for hands!—I'll never lift a finger."[29]

As one of the hotheaded young travelers of the poem, Serge was much closer in spirit to Rimbaud *le voyou* in his nihilistic rebelliousness. In his maturity, however, Serge came to sympathize with the very sorts of people he had scorned before.[30] The values of friendship, community, and solidarity in adversity, and the feeling for the inviolability of the individual deeply inform his poetry and his resistance to totalitarianism. And if Serge often resorts to religious imagery and language, he does so to use their numinous power to address human suffering, not to invoke a deity—Serge's spirituality is of this world. In this poem, the Russian church and the Mexican church, while fulfilling their traditional roles as providers of solace, function also as objective correlatives to Serge's perennial outsider status. And for Serge the churches are emotional vantage points on the still-living, turbulent histories of the Russian and the Mexican revolutions.

At the Russian church situated on "snowy plains . . . under a splendidly dazzling sun," all is bright, clear, and peaceful, and Serge and his delighted companions are relieved of their inner turmoil in the vicissitudes of revolution. Under the sign of the crimson flame, these young people mentally and emotionally afflicted by "obsessive suns" of their ideas and ideals are momentarily restored to themselves and the ordinary social world. But theirs is an ephemeral reconciliation, a northern analogue of the dreamed-of peaceful islands of "Tête-à-Tête" and "Song."

In Mexico many years later, "after the wars revolutions mass graves inexplicable crimes," Serge comes upon the church "with the black flame." As if it were the photographic negative of the Russian church, the church at San Juan Parangaricutiro is set in a landscape that seems to contain "the most immense battlefields of our times," where nature is ripping itself apart as the Paricutín volcano engulfs the town with ash, lava, and "dark destructive snow cosmic dust cold fire dust." Unlike the Russian church, which was blessed by a clear winter's day, the Mexican church has "slipped into the irreconcilable night / a night of annihilation"—into utter hell on "the inhuman earth," where the dark plume of the volcano blots out the stars.

In the 22 February 1943 entry of *Carnets*, Serge mentions reading the news of the sudden appearance of the volcano: a man "working in his fields saw the earth slowly rise, 'as if it were breathing,' and smoke and sparks issuing from little crevices." [31] Serge then follows a chain of meaningful coincidences that link the volcano with his dream of an earthquake, with real earthquakes, and with cosmic catastrophes and social chaos. As if he were beginning a Surrealist narrative of chance encounters, [32] Serge writes, "For me, it all began with a dream" in which he sees a crowded building split in two. An earthquake strikes a couple of days later, and Serge happens upon a destroyed building that resembles the one in his dream.

Discussing all this with his friend Fritz Fränkel, a German psychoanalyst and revolutionary who had participated in Walter Benjamin's drug experiments, Serge remarks that he has used the word "earthquake" (*séisme*) several times in his writings to characterize great events and that his latest novel includes a seismologist. Realizing that the psychoanalytic mechanism of repression was in operation, Serge writes that in the conversation he forgot to connect the seismologist to the working title of the novel, *La Terre commence à trembler* (The Earth Begins to Shake), published as *The Case of Comrade Tulayev*.[33] As if to complete the series of deep images that appear in much of his fiction and poetry, Serge confesses his love of looking at the night sky, even though he always expected to see portents of disaster there—perhaps an exploding star that would fill the sky with fire.

Late that night another earthquake occurs, rousing Serge and his family from sleep. Serge comments on experiencing an "animal panic" mixed with a feeling of powerlessness at the core of his being, as if the earth were floating and mountains were breaking up. The next morning, Serge remarks to Fränkel that they are "like the people of the Middle Ages who, amid the social chaos, fed on the Apocalypse as they awaited the Millennium." When Serge eventually visited San Juan Parangaricutiro and the Paricutín volcano, his dreams came true.[34]

As "Mexico: Churches" unfolds at the volcano and in town, Serge and his companions take reassurance from the dignity of some Indios "eating tortillas in the halos of smoky lamps / —what calm ruled there what security in calm and certain destruction." The oxymoronic linking of "calm" and "certain destruction" in this fiery dark night of the soul already indicates the path to take: the next morning is "as calm with annihilation as the night of annihilation" as the Indios drag themselves on their knees into "the transparently bright nave" of the church.

Amid the darkness and the destruction, Serge finds a corollary to the Russian church: the black flame of the Mexican church sheds its unique light not only on the natural disaster but also on the destruction of so much of what Serge holds dear. In the days when the Bolshevik revolution still held promise of a better, more just life, the young Serge and his friends experienced a moment of personal reconciliation in the Russian church. By the time Serge is in exile in Mexico, his world and his hopes are in ruins. The reconciliation that he needs must be collective and communal, and thus objective. The Indios also arrive at the church from historical disasters, including the genocide of the Spanish Conquest and the ambiguous results of the Mexican Revolution.[35]

The Indios do not so much fight the catastrophe as fuse with it: they are "men of energy and ash," people of the earth whose rites in the nominally Catholic church long predate European contact as they perform a strange hopping dance before the altar. As in "Death of Panait," with its death-knell repetition of "finished," "Mexico: Churches" uses the repetition of a phrase in part for its sound: *réconciliés avec*—"reconciled with"—seems to echo the "murmured prayers and the scuffing sound" of the worshippers' feet on the stones, to insist on the need for absolute reconciliation of the victims with their fate:

> reconciled with the disaster
> reconciled with the death throes of the land under
>   basaltic fire and ash
> reconciled with the end of the world—and why not?
> reconciled
>
> Thy will be done oh Lord—oh Planet!

Serge and his companions are not of the place, not "men of energy and ash," yet they are participants, not spectators, in the rites they witness. Even though the pious worshippers ignore the strangers, Serge insists that "we saw them we understood them deeply through a sort of transparence." In "Mexico: Churches" this membrane of transparency joins more than it separates, and to be "reconciled with the end of the world" is in effect to be reconciled with the world: the natural world, the social world, and the world at war.[36] It is also to be reconciled with oneself, even for a torn man of Eurasia. Concealed and revealed in the images of disaster is the prospect of regeneration, of a world created anew out of the raw materials of "dark destructive snow cosmic dust cold fire dust."

Serge wrote "Hands" the day before he died.[37] Timing alone does not make the poem a kind of accidental epitaph: with its intimations of mortality and its foregrounding of communication, continuity, and connection through art, "Hands" extends the themes of reconciliation and transparency found in "Mexico: Churches" while also hinting at Serge's ars poetica.

A piece of sculpture, which Serge might have seen reproduced in an art book, is the pretext for the poem. The poet, reaching across "from one end of time to another," addresses an anonymous man who was the model for the terra-cotta sculpture by a sixteenth-century Italian artist, "nameless like you":

> What astonishing contact, old man, your hands
> establish with our own!
> How vain the centuries of death next to your hands . . .

Serge looks back in time through the present tense of the writing of the poem. The sculptor is faceless as well as nameless, and Serge himself is almost anonymous behind the pronoun "I." Interestingly, the contact he seeks is not with the artist but with the old man who is the artist's model, whose hands of another time and place implore a response, not from God but from other men and women:

> The veins of your hands, old man, express prayer,
> the prayer of your blood, old man, the next-to-last prayer,
> not verbal prayer, not clerical prayer,
> but the prayer of reasoning fervor,
> powerful—powerless.
> Their presence confronts the world with itself . . .

This opening of communication between Serge and the old man invites the readers of "Hands" to join with them as witness-participants. As if echoing the relationship between Serge and the Indios in "Mexico: Churches," here Serge and the old man do not see us, the readers; we are nonetheless brought into the drama of the poem through "a sort of transparence." Serge returns the invitation to profane prayer by "throwing onto the inexorable scales of the universe / at least the fragility of a thought, a sign, a line of verse" that is "as real as the imploring veins of your hand, / as real as the veins of mine so little different."

That the representation of the old man's hands in the sculpture and then in the poem "confronts the world with itself" brings readers closer to the world as well. For Serge, these imagined points of contact are not merely the result of plays of appearance within the poem: against all odds, something essential is transmitted as Serge and the old man discover what they have in common:

> A drop of blood—
> a single shaft of light falls from one hand to the other,
> dazzling.

In this image of essential, elemental solidarity between one man and another across turbulent centuries, "Hands" also intimates Serge's model of poetry—and a model for how to read his poetry. Whatever else we find in his poetry, we are meant to find him and his world, which despite everything is also our world, and this for Serge is another kind of transparency: a hard-won transparency of communication through the language of poetry.

Notes

1   Serge was born Victor Kibalchich. For more about the background to the poetry, see Richard Greeman, "Afterword: The Odyssey of a Revolutionary Poet," in this book. Serge tells his story in *Memoirs of a Revolutionary*, Peter Sedgwick with George Paizis, trans. (New York: New York Review Books, 2012). For an appreciation of Serge's

novels in their political, philosophical, and literary contexts, see Bill Marshall, *Victor Serge: The Uses of Dissent* (Berg: New York, 1992). For a fascinating look at the Paris of the young Victor Serge, see Luc Sante, *The Other Paris* (New York: Farrar, Straus and Giroux, 2015).

2   Victor Serge, "Souvenirs," 28 février 1943, in *Carnets (1936–1947)*, édition établie par Claudio Albertani et Claude Rioux (Marseille: Agone, 2012), 280. Serge's working title for his memoirs was *Souvenirs des mondes disparus* (Memories of Bygone Worlds).

3   Jean Rière gave *Messages* its first publication in his edition of Victor Serge, *Pour un brasier dans un désert* (Bassac [Charente], France: Plein Chant, 1998), which also includes *Résistance*, "Mains," and other poems.

4   Serge, *Memoirs*, 21.

5   Mitchell Abidor, "Editor's Introduction: The Old Mole of Individual Freedom," in Victor Serge, *Anarchists Never Surrender: Essays, Polemics, and Correspondence on Anarchism, 1908–1938*, Mitchell Abidor, ed. and trans. (Oakland, CA: PM Press, 2015), 1.

6   See especially Walt Whitman, *Drum-Taps: The Complete 1865 Edition*, Lawrence Kramer, ed. (New York: New York Review Books, 2015). Whitman's Civil War poems are in some ways precursors of Serge's elegies for friends and comrades lost in rebellion, revolution, civil war, and counterrevolution.

7   In this essay, I focus on only a handful of Serge's characteristic themes and images in hopes of bringing readers closer to the poetry. I mean to suggest openings, not to present conclusions.

8   Marshall holds that "the personal courage and authenticity" of André Gide "probably inspired the figure of Félicien Mûrier" (*Victor Serge*, 95).

9   Victor Serge, *The Long Dusk*, Ralph Manheim, trans. (New York: The Dial Press, 1946), 153.

10   Victor Serge, *The Case of Comrade Tulayev*, Willard R. Trask, trans. (Garden City, NY: Doubleday, 1950), 293–294.

11   Wallace Stevens, *Collected Poetry and Prose* (New York: Library of America, 1997), 285–286. I owe my discovery of the Serge–Stevens connection to D. L. Macdonald's intriguing discussion in "Wallace Stevens and Victor Serge," *Dalhousie Review* 66, nos. 1–2 (Spring–Summer 1986): 174–180. Macdonald notes that Stevens would have read translated excerpts from *Memoirs of a Revolutionary* in Dwight Macdonald's *Politics* magazine. The Konstantinov episode is in Victor Serge, "The Revolution at Dead-End (1926–1928)," Ethel Libson, trans., *Politics* 1, no. 5 (June 1944): 147–151. The current translation of the episode is in Serge, *Memoirs*, 236–240.

12   Serge, *Memoirs*, 238–239.

13 Stevens, *Collected Poetry*, 174. Alan Filreis discusses Stevens, left politics, and poetry in relation to this poem and others in "Stevens in the 1930s," in John N. Serio, ed., *The Cambridge Companion to Wallace Stevens* (Cambridge: Cambridge University Press, 2007), 41–42.

14 A snapshot taken on board the *Capitaine Paul-Lemerle* shows Serge standing next to Breton's wife, Jacqueline Lamba, with Lam and his wife, Helena Holzer, to their right. See the photo archives of the United States Holocaust Museum at http://digitalassets.ushmm. org/photoarchives/detail.aspx?id=1155267. The notes to the photograph provide background information. (Thanks to Anna Pravdová for directing me to this photograph.) Breton kept a signed copy of *Résistance*, as well as copies of Serge's *Vie des révolutionnaires*, *Seize fusillés*, and *Portrait de Staline*, till the end of his life in 1966. See the inventory of his collection at http://www.andrebreton.fr.

15 Interview with Octavio Paz in Rita Guibert, *Seven Voices: Seven Latin American Writers Talk to Rita Guibert*, Frances Partridge, trans. (New York: Vintage Books, 1973), 214; Octavio Paz, *Itinerary: An Intellectual Journey*, Jason Wilson, trans. (New York: Harcourt, 1999), 52–53.

16 Serge, "Surréalisme," 2 janvier 1942, *Carnets*, 156–159. Although Michaux was not a member of the Surrealist group, he was close to Surrealism. The title of Michaux's poem is "Contre," translated as "Counter" in Henri Michaux, *Selected Writings: The Space Within*, Richard Ellmann, trans. (New York: New Directions Books, 1968), 125–127.

17 See Serge, "The Writer's Conscience" [1947], in David Craig, ed., *Marxists on Literature: An Anthology* (Harmondsworth: Penguin Books, 1975), 435–444, and Benjamin Péret, *Le Déshonneur des poètes*, précédé de *La Parole est à Péret*, préface de Jean Schuster (Paris: Jean-Jacques Pauvert, 1965), 82. Péret critiques *L'Honneur des poètes* (The Honor of the Poets), a collection of Resistance poems.

18 Serge, "Lac de Pátzcuaro – Giraudoux," 22–27 février 1944, *Carnets*, 475. The English translation of the complete line is by J. H. Matthews, from "Lobster," in Benjamin Péret, *Péret's Score* (Paris: Lettres Modernes, 1965), 41.

19 Serge, "Surréalisme," 2 janvier 1942, *Carnets*, 158–159. Serge was provoked by a comment that Jacqueline Lamba made on the first line of "Sunday" (*Messages*): "The singer was singing oh life is so beautiful." Lamba's criticism: "The correct word isn't poetry. I would have written: 'The singer was sleeping . . .'"

20 Kenneth Rexroth, *The Complete Poems of Kenneth Rexroth*, Sam Hamill and Bradford Murrow, eds. (Port Townsend, WA: Copper Canyon Press, 2003), 154–155. Such poems are complemented by

the wry, despairing "New Objectives, New Cadres" (158), whose satire of Bolshevik "purer logic" is closer to Stevens—as well as to Yevgeny Zamyatin's dystopian novel, *We*.

21 Kenneth Rexroth, "Victor Serge's Memoirs of a Revolutionary," *San Francisco Examiner*, 8 September 1963, on Ken Knabb's Bureau of Public Secrets site at http://bopsecrets.org/rexroth/sfe/1963/09.htm#Victor-Serge.

22 The allusion is to the title of Philip Levine's *The Names of the Lost*, with its moving elegies to anarchists who died in the Spanish Civil War. Thanks to Christopher Winks, a fellow member of the not entirely imaginary Serge International, for reminding me of Levine's book, whose poetry has much in common with Serge's.

23 Compare this movement toward reconciliation with Rexroth's long poem on the death of Dylan Thomas, "Thou Shalt Not Kill," which continually rises in fury at Thomas's presumed murderers to conclude with the sea birds of New York harbor screaming, "You killed him! You killed him. / In your God damned Brooks Brothers suit, / You son of a bitch." The poem seems less an elegy than a sort of reverse panegyric in which Thomas is praised by condemning all others. Rexroth, *Complete Poems*, 573.

24 Serge, *Memoirs*, 323.

25 Panaït Istrati, *Vers l'autre flamme, après seize mois dans l'U.R.S.S.: Confession pour vaincus* (Paris: Gallimard, 1987), with additional documents.

26 Serge, *Memoirs*, 321–322.

27 This list includes terms that Anselm Jappe uses to describe Serge under the less dynamic rubric of "his background hesitation": "son hésitation de fond entre anarchisme et bolchevisme, individualisme et collectivisme, littérature et action" (Anselm Jappe, "Postface," in Eleni Samios-Kazantzaki, *La Véritable tragédie de Panaït Istrati* [Fécamp, France: Nouvelles Éditions Lignes, 2013], 302). The book, whose main text is a memoir of the Panait Istrati–Nikos Kazantzakis tour of the Soviet Union in 1927–1928, includes 43 letters from Serge to Istrati. Marshall stresses "the dialectical aspect of [Serge's] thought" in dealing with "the dynamic confrontations of seemingly irreconcilable positions" (*Victor Serge*, 7).

28 Marshall, *Victor Serge*, 111–114, discusses Serge's frequent use of images of volcanism and earthquake in his literary works, including in "Le Séisme" (The Earthquake), published in Victor Serge, *Le Tropique et le nord: L'hôpital de Léningrad et autres nouvelles* (Paris: François Maspéro, 1972); "Le Séisme" was written during the same period as "Mexico: Churches." In a perhaps telling coincidence, Stevens's "Esthétique du Mal" opens in the shadow of Vesuvius, which "had groaned / For a month" (*Complete Poems*, 277).

29 Rimbaud's influence is apparent in Serge's novel *Men in Prison*, in which a chapter titled "Drunken Boat" narrates the prisoner's descent into the endless, dark time of incarceration (Richard Greeman, trans. [Oakland, CA: PM Press, 2014]). Likewise, passages in some of Serge's poems (e.g., "The rats are leaving . . .," "Caribbean Sea," and "Our Children") seem to respond directly to Rimbaud's poem "The Drunken Boat."

30 See Abidor, "Editor's Introduction," in Serge, *Anarchists Never Surrender*, 12–14.

31 Serge, "La Terre tremble," 22 février 1943, *Carnets*, 276–280. The story is expanded on in Serge, "Le Séisme."

32 Notwithstanding his objections to Surrealism, Serge swims in the same waters here, with his interest in psychoanalysis and his abiding need to reconcile the contraries of his existence.

33 Moreover, the words Serge uses to describe the birth of the Paricutín volcano are very similar to the words he uses in *The Case of Comrade Tulayev* to describe the birth of "another idea"—one that replaces the idea of justice—that comes to Romachkin during a sordid sexual encounter with a prostitute: "At that instant, another idea was born in him. Feeble, faraway, hesitant, not wanting to live, it yet was born. Thus from volcanic soil rises a tiny flame, which, small though it may be, yet reveals that the earth will quake and crack and burst with flowing lava" (7).

34 See the following entries in Serge, *Carnets*: "Paricutín," 22 août 1943, 385–388; "Dr Atl" [undated], 388–393; and "Paricutín," 20–27 février 1944, 477–479. Dr. Atl was the pseudonym of the painter Gerardo Murillo, a veteran of the Mexican Revolution who was obsessed with volcanoes.

35 Serge notes that their church was "a symbol of submission before it became a symbol of faith" ("Le Séisme," 33).

36 Writing near the end of his life, Serge laments "our time of cessation of war without peace, that is to say, without reconciliation of the victims, without a reconstruction of the world, without renewal of our confidence in man" ("The Writer's Conscience," 435).

37 For Vlady's note on the circumstances of Serge's death, see Greeman, "Afterword."

I. Resistance

Note

With the exception of four pieces in the same spirit that were written in Petrograd in 1920–1928 or recently in Paris, I have here collected the poems I wrote in Russia in 1935–1936 during the period of deportation that I spent in Orenburg: I had to recreate them later, since the Soviet censorship did not allow me to take any of my manuscripts with me.

To my companions in captivity in 1933–1936,
Boris Eltsin, Pevzner, Chernykh, Belenky, Byk,
Lakovitsky, Santalov, Lydia Svalova, Fayna Upstein,
Left Communists,

Nesterov and Yegorich, Right Communists,

without knowing whether my thoughts find them alive or dead,

but with the certainty that alive or dead,
whether resisters or victims of torture,
these men and women remain,
in the shipwrecked revolution,
examples of complete and lucid fidelity
to the true revolution.

Another will smash the prison register.
Another will smash the doors of the jail.
Another will wipe from our thin shoulders
The dust and blood fallen from our necks.

—Péguy

Frontier

Banks of the Ural,
The woods are turning silver, the river dozes on the sands,
the kite bird soars—
yet not so high as the pursuit plane
that jauntily loops the loop of death at the edge of the
    golden fringes of a white cloud
and, at times, at the very edge
of a terrestrial abyss deeper than the stellar abyss.

Here ends Europe, frontier of a world
for which the Atlantic is only an inland sea and Atlantis a
    vague recollection.
7 a.m., it's 8 p.m. at the other end of Greater Europe,
in Frisco, San Francisco, at the edge of the Pacific, on the
    frontier of the next, Greater War,
Frisco where the IWWs live.
What eyes straining toward Asia peer at the Ocean over
    there,
eyes sad like mine from sounding this tangible void where
    continents begin and end,
through the silence of the other human face?

The steppe begins with innocent plains,
with the purity of plains, the fertility, the immensity of
    plains
and this contact of bare earth offered to the clouds.
Free attraction of spheres, space,
red colts galloping toward the spring of springs.

The vanquished wheat fields come to an end, the sand
    dunes rise,
a scarlet sun brutally consumes them,
oh thirst, eternity, conflagration, bones,
vanity of vanities!

The Kirghiz camel driver has stopped singing—
immobile, blazing madness of the sand,
mirages—when will the stars come out, but do they even
    exist?
Will the mildness of just one evening ever come again,
the cool of just one night,
the unbelievable kindness of a stagnant pond for the camel
    driver's throat,
for the dog's rough tongue,
for the camel's tortured mouth?

Silence absorbs the expanse.

The primordial clay is coral red,
the sun drives home its dreadful red nails,
and this is where people saw a strange crimson beast running,
spurred on by all the earth's suffering.
Its enormous flanks blocked out the entire horizon.

(And you know, the earth suffers more than hell,
hell was never more than a delirious mirage
of the children of the earth.)

When the Uzbek hunter, the flock's good avenger,
takes a wolf alive, he ties it up and, singing to himself,
slowly flays it, taking good care
to avoid the arteries;

he flays it and then he hurls it across the steppe.
People claim
that an expertly flayed wolf can run for quite some time
across the bloody desert,
running and running toward a miraculous stream in the
    Kara-Kum Desert,
a Milky Way,
a place to quench its unimaginable thirst.

The mirage magnifies its looming image
wobbling
above the still-smoking lava of chaos.
Shepherd's eyes enclose this image in legend forever,
a legend I am drafting on the frontier of Asia,
on the frontier of Europe,
I who feel like a torn man of Eurasia.

People of the Ural

In winter the people of this land keep warm by burning the
    kiziak
they make from cow pats gathered on the steppe and dried
    in the sun,
and it's an ancient task for woman and beast.
Elsewhere, beautiful laughing women stomp ripe grapes
and the wine fumes make them a little drunk, but they do
    not know they have sisters here.
Vast, vast horizons, pure distant weightless,
soft grass whence rises a shimmering heat,
vast, vast forgotten sky, a blinding sky one no longer sees,
a slender, bare-legged Tatiana stands there, slowly turning
    in the warm manure
and the cow also turns at the end of its tether, woman and
    animal together, sweating,
strangers to the horizon.
Blue-black flies buzz around them in the stench,
the breathing of the animal is weary like a plaint.
The young woman stops now and then and sings softly to
    herself from the depths of her misery
that when the man came back from a distant prison
and found the woman he loved in bed with another man he
    killed them both with a blow of his ax—
now her voice turns gently heartrending:
Othello!
and it is only the complaint of Bogdan the Convict,
last spring the story took place in a neighboring village,
the spring before that in another,
this is a story for all seasons,
"for in this world all men kill the thing they love . . ."
Dust, dust lies on Desdemona,
yet a naked breast makes life bloom . . .

Then there's the fisherman in the pond,
a bony old man in this sparkling water
who is poorer than the poor man in Puvis's gray landscape.
Naked save for his short jacket and shepherd's felt hat,
he waded in to draw the net: "Hey! Hey! Damn it, Kolka,
    you too—pull harder, damn it!"
The slender naked child was struggling on the far bank.
Live silvery commas suddenly quivered about their feet in
    the mud.
"Get them, get them, boy!"
Lord, there is nothing miraculous about this draft of fishes,
    the miracle, Lord, is that anyone can live on it!

Red granite shows through the red clay,
the world's first days show through the sorrow of life,
the street sets off, squeezed between its tottering, tumble-
    down houses like old women squatting in the sun,
it claims scant space between sky and endless steppe,
a ragged Kirghiz man walks alone, glumly pursued by the
    barking of dogs,
nothing to steal, nothing to eat, filthy beggar! and even the
    dogs know you are hungry . . .
I met his black look from the depths of time,
he has gone past, he is the past.

Here I am at my table, with a few pages begun,
tense pages
that would like to live and already feel lost, alone before
    these
stifled pages
with this ton of lead on the back of my neck and my worries.
Ah, what is happening in Asturias?
Let's get to work. The naked fisherman dragging his net in
    the pond did not see the patches of sky I saw there.

Let's get to work so that one day a passerby might see
in the lines taking form at this moment, as I too draw my
    net in the pond of useless days,
patches of a clearing sky I cannot see in them . . .

(O[renburg], Summer [19]35.)

Old Woman

This old woman walking under a yoke
loaded with unspeakable things
casts a shadow like the caricature of a horse,
a poor old nag
whose head hangs only by a wire.

The ancients disputed whether such beings had a soul,
immortal or not.
Barely equipped with one themselves, scholars
gravely pondered the question.

Today, plaster saints and others
would in lyrical terms call you sister.
Old woman,
you do not even suspect their comfortable lie,
it is a thousand million leagues away
from your heavy, dull steps stamped on the black earth.

The truth spatters beneath your steps
in your wet shadow
reeking of manure.

You can no longer be saved.
Just think! Seventy years old,
it is too late.
And perhaps six hundred and seventy years of servitude
or more.
It is too early.

Somewhere else . . .

Midnight, and I am smoking under the shed whose roof is
   corroded by snow.
The Milky Way shines through the cracks.
Around this squatting woman move giant shadows of old
   servants,
serfs who were whipped, who were sold . . .
She has powerful, tenacious hands that in the darkness
   work the desolate whiteness,
that have worked hard, stubbornly,
since the beginning of time,
crushing with light taps the chalk she will knead into shape
   near dawn.
The granite vibrates slightly under the muffled blows,
isn't this the beating of the exhausted old heart of this land?

I speak aloud, between long intervals of silence, words
   almost devoid of sense
to fill the void between us, old woman,
the void of appearances,
because under my breath I tell you things that surprise me,
   things you could not understand.
If Orion's Belt suddenly fell to earth in a shower of burning
   stars,
wouldn't you think the end of the world had come?
"Lord, have mercy on our fields!
All these falling stars will only bring people more bad luck!"

Somewhere else, grandmother,
there are women who are gracious, perfumed, pampered,
   loved, loving,
they will never know anything of your pain, your hunger,
   these shadows where you toil—

there are elegant men with eloquent gestures who speak to
    them
of the Oedipus complex, the aesthetic sense, conscience,
    and even of the proletariat;
somewhere tonight there is a happy Angelita—
    "Querida Angelita, amiga mía, tanto querida!"
    Sweet Angelita, my darling, my beloved!

Somewhere else . . .
This grandmother answers me in her rough voice, worn out
    by swamp fevers,
that you can't get the good crumbly chalk you used to,
that the waters of the Sakmara are going to overflow and
    fields will get flooded,
that life is hard, always hard—no, you have no idea how
    long life goes on!
And her hands
work, work, work
for all eternity.

Just Four Girls

Four girls wade gaily into the water to ford the Ural,
the sparkling, shimmering, life-giving water.
The water grasps the firm calves of these walkers from the
    edge of the steppes,
an invisible caressing hand discreetly
takes their knees, then a brisk coolness
weds their legs and rises to brush their secret flesh,
making short shrill laughter tremble on their lips,
a laughter
whose taste is like that of a bitter fruit
in the mouth of a thirsty man.
Under her little red calico dress the first one stretches her
    young body, a sketch
of an Athenian Victory with her slightly pointed breasts.
She has hair cut short on the nape, a high forehead, one
    arm outstretched,
the hand horizontal, and that already strong hand of a
    hardworking virgin
seems to point toward a summit,
an island,
a city
on the other side of the world, where all is but "order,
beauty,
luxury, calm, and voluptuousness"
—but she is only pointing the way to a linden rustling with
    nests
on the other bank.
Will she, a serf barely freed, poorly freed, ever know
how to put a name to beauty,
she who so clearly sees the calm landscape of which she is
at this moment
the youthful living heart?

Another girl, thickset, has the shoulders of a
     sixteen-year-old,
making one think of the graceful ungainliness of animals,
of colorful shawls, furs under a tent of animal hides.
She must have very dark little eyes, without lids, almost
     without brows,
the white close-set teeth of a carnivore,
her flat face looks firm, hard, with round cheekbones.
In the thirteenth century Hulagu Khan's archers had the
     same cheekbones,
teeth, dark eyes, guarded smile as this child
when they forded the river, coming the other way,
in triumph.

The last two girls laugh as they stumble against each other,
sisters, friends, pals, I cannot see their faces.
They arch their backs amid the green reflections of the
     foliage.
What festival, what love, what desire, what pleasure are they
     talking about to inspire that tinkling laughter?
Probably none; in them it's
just the laughter of a fine day.
I will not see them again except in other girls, I will not
     recognize them
if I see them dancing one evening to a brass band.
They probably are not beautiful, they probably have no
     special charm,
no more genius than a blossoming flower,
no more pride,
no more kindness.
(But is any more needed?)
They are just four girls among all the others, like all the
     others, four human figurines
molded by the moment,
released from the common fate and returning to it
as if to a lover.

I know they will not have their promised joy,
happiness is not on the other side of the river,
the other face of the world will stay closed to them,
their future has the dull color of the plains.

Far away now, almost gone, where are they,
the four laughing girls of a moment ago?

They are on the other bank, four real girls
from my village of exile,
and in me their image has not faded.

The Asphyxiated Man

The green shrubs are bursting, there are these giant flowers,
in the doorway of the little gray-board surgical hospital
there are these dormant flowers
that smack of chloroform.

A young nurse in white sits on the steps,
she is a brunette with the wide eyes of the plains,
she is crunching sunflower seeds between her teeth.

The patient, squatting on the ground, in an oversize shirt,
where his unsung martyr's body wobbles,
cranes his bony neck; his face is a strange gray color,
he looks like a man badly drowned, badly fished out, badly
    dispatched,
it is the face of asphyxiation, the face of the terror
of the last days,
pierced by eyes prior to any resurrection.

His hoarse breathing disturbs the buzzing flies,
I see the veins throb in his neck.
His otherworldly eyes cry out to me that there is no more
    air,

"Citizen! What have they done with all the air of the earth?"

Two high-breasted girls stop before this asphyxiated man.
The one who wears a sailor's jacket, with an anchor and a
    lover's name tattooed on her bare arm,
and who has close-cropped hair and sensual pink nostrils,
says to her friend:
"Oh my, he's had it, girl, death is written all over his face!"
She puts an arm around her friend's thin shoulders and
    says: "Let's go, Charlotte!"

The flier who parachuted at dawn from seventh heaven
and who knows there is air you can drown in, air you can
      smash up in, air, air you can fall through,
kilometers of air and terror to traverse with a cool head
either to die or to get your certificate, first-class rations, and
      a knowledge of the sky that is only fresh ignorance of
      the heavens—
the flier's eyes follow the young women,
"No one can do anything for the poor old guy now, no point
      even looking at him, let's go, my lovelies."

He would like to dance tonight in Linden Gardens
with the tattooed girl whose nostrils are sensual and pink,
he would suddenly clutch her breasts in his hands
"Ah, you're a great kid, I can buy you silk stockings, you
      know,
we're the happy youth of the birth of socialism."

—Believers say that a Christ died on the cross for you
that is not so clear.
The Savior botched your salvation.

The speakers at the Atheists Club say revolutions were
      made to save you and people like you
—that is even less clear,

and yet all those important people, all those healthy people
are quite positive.

Your papers prove that you fought to save yourself
with Chapayev, with Furmanov, with my friend Mitia the
      deported wino,
along the Ural River stripped bare by the dawn—
but even that did you little good.

And your blood burning from the civil wars, the rage in
    your partisan hearts,
all that would be lost, poor people, if there were not good
    authors,
servile glory hounds, astute moneymakers
to crank out memorable books and screenplays about it.

The nurse has finished crunching her seeds, she has gone
    away.
The asphyxiated man remains alone amid the green shrubs
in the dazzling light and colors and pain,
alone in the whole universe,
alone in the pure inaccessible unbreathable azure,
where his black mouth begs in vain for air.

Luminous disks descend, ascend, explode there
and I am here, dressed in white, eyes framed in gold, useless,
I the solitary consciousness of his suffering and his death,
I the last, powerless human face this man will ever see,
I who have nothing to offer him but an absurd remorse.

O[renburg], Summer [19]35.

Tiflis

Kurdish women in red dresses, a little donkey ambling
    down the back street of the Maidan,
chance colors, their capricious fits of sleep, their waking
    amid the bazaar's shifting arabesques,
copper necklaces around the necks of little barbarian girls,
    little Tartars
who sell ripe grapes and fiery peppers,
the steam from the scalding water surging from
    underground lava flows
for the Orbeliani baths, pay three rubles and be pure.

Two short-legged oxen, stocky and stubborn, part the
    crowd, their gray horns thrust forward,
they patiently draw the old two-wheeled cart from the time
    of Tamerlane.
A man dressed in homespun drives them, he is stocky like
    them, stubborn like them, this man from Mingrelia,
the only difference is that he can sing Rustaveli's verses.

In the Blue Mosque of Shah Abbas, covered in radiant
    faience,
an anonymous captive walked briskly between unsheathed
    sabers,
preceded by an invisible hope.
His sandals trod the dust, and so they might have trodden
    the foamy crests of the sea.

From the square windows of the Metekh prison, the faces of
    the earth nearest heaven
apparently
could see him go,
go and come back.

The Georgian tombs of the Monastery of Saint David lie on
the border between presence and the void,
these paving stones of flesh-toned alabaster endlessly
release
so much carnal coolness that they truly bear witness to
eternal life,
where the name, the face, the suffering, and even the
memory of a person fade away.

From the heights of Mount David I saw the glaciers of
Elbrus, Kazbek, and farther off, icier, more limpid,
Ararat, Pamir, Everest, the Andes, and farther off, icier,
more limpid,
above the gently oscillating green fields the dazzling
summits of the truest mountains:
these are the nameless mountains of the only necessary
continents
—oh absolute deserts, oh fertile continents of consent and
refusal!

O[renburg], 1935.

Crime in Tiflis

Ah, why was he drinking Imeritia wine,
that man with the bag of silver who came from Kutaisi,
with his old heart trodden on like a Kurdish carpet
on which people have haggled so much, suffered, danced,
trampled on promises, and stabbed someone
so poorly loved, on which people have so soundly slept?

Why did he fancy the girl whose heartrending song
lied like all of life, tempted like all of night?

He would rather have fallen into rivers of stars,
oh cool Milky Way, Andromeda, Pleiades, Cassiopeia!
fallen toward you, to be no more than falling, bursting,
    flowing, calm,
but he fell with the weight of flesh, pain, and the grave,
through the narrow window, just thirty meters, his aorta
    lightly pierced.

The phosphorescent waters foamed in the depths of the
    drowned firmament,
they washed his wounds, they swept along his body so
    treacherously crushed.
But in the morning
the Tamaras were rinsing their laundry on the banks of the
    Kura,
these lovers with childlike eyes had supple arms that the
    waters caressed more than love ever did,
it was into the depths of their eyes that the murdered man
    fell, for they believed they recognized him without
    knowing him,
they mourned him without loving him, laid him in the
    ground, then smiled at the living and soon forgot him.

O[renburg], 1935.

Russian History

I. *Alexis Mikhaylovich*

Czar Alexis Mikhaylovich, the very silent,
the very gentle,
the very pious,
would wash his hand after a foreigner had kissed it.

The chronicle reports that like a good Christian he fasted
three days out of seven.
All the same, he died obese after ordering a fair amount of
   torture
like a gentle czar.

He is depicted with a tawny beard, a healthy complexion, a
   smooth brow,
a fleeting reddish glint in his cunning eyes,
under a pointed hat with a white fur trim.
He loved pearls, brocade, Isfahan silks,
gold, silver, precious stones;
once a year he threw a banquet for the poor.
Poor folk, may your wounds redeem his sins
of evil thoughts, lust, gluttony,
and a few superfluous massacres.
God knows most of them are justified and that I am a
   merciful czar.
Poor folk, even if you know he is lying,
eat and drink your fill, if your wounds
did not serve to redeem the powerful, what else would they
   be good for?

He chose a wife from among the loveliest girls in the land.
Intrigue dumped before this fearsome fiancé a pale Ophelia
half-strangled by her braids.

Her father was deported because of the hope, fear, and
    mortal anguish
the virgin had suffered.
Intrigue brought him pure-hearted Natalya
whose belly would carry hard-hearted little Peter
—father unknown.
He was a better husband and a better father than the great
    czar Ivan Vasilyevich the Terrible
and his own nominal son Peter Alekseyevich the Great
because none of his children died by his own hand
and he had none of his wives put to the torture.

If he exiled his favorites, was that not the custom?
If he exiled the incorruptible patriarch and the steadfast
    heresiarch,
was that done without love?
If he had heretics burned in the northern forests,
was that not out of love?

Let us respect in him the wise politician
educated by riot,
the perspicacious monarch who, in his secret tête-à-tête
    with fright,
had long discovered the surest resources of power:

fear, denunciation, betrayal, espionage,
the moderate torture of strappado,
exile and deportation
to the polar regions, to the ends of the earth,
and he knew how to build in the dark mire of the human
    heart
his Chancellery of Secret Affairs,
an exemplary institution, all in all, oh Holy Office!

Perhaps his financial deals,
adroitly clinched with hangings,

were unfortunate
and slightly redolent of counterfeiting,
inflation, bankruptcy et cetera,
—but were not all great kings, the Lord's Anointed,
great counterfeiters?

In short, all he needed to go down as a monarch of the first
    order
was to have been a little more intelligent,
a little better served,
a little more wicked,
and to have had a little less need of cash.

II. *Stenka Razin*

In those days there lived, made powerful through sword,
    fire, blood,
Another czar, the one they called the czar of the brigands.
All along the Volga, our mother, he lighted
The signal fires of a wild deliverance, bristling with scythes,
Gallows, and severed heads.

Liberty, equality, fraternity,
Name the fruits of the most bitter hope,
Wash, wash away from the knives, from the swords
The blood shed since the beginning of time.
Stenka the Just knew to treat the masters
As masters treat the slaves
And he never imagined that a better man might emerge.
In the evenings the Cossack girls in this village still sing
The complaint of Stenka Razin
To the accompaniment of a guitar; but what their fathers
And their uncles did, right here, a mere sixteen years ago,
They have forgotten, let's forget it, guitar,
Sing for their hearts,

Enchant oblivion, make the choirs
Harmonized by oblivion sing.

A silver sickle rises in the July sky
Above the little red minaret of Orenpossad.
I listen to these thin voices and the guitar
And the toads croaking in the pond.
Alone before the steppe, I think obscurely
Of all those the world over from whom I am nowise
    separated,
Of the unemployed in Amsterdam, of Tom Mooney in his
    California prison
For fifteen or eighteen years now, what do we know about
    that?
And who knows the true toll of such years?
Of the astonishing victory of the Saragossa general strike
    yesterday,
In June 1934,
Of the next Congress of the United Federation of Teachers,
Of the fresh grave—but are there flowers on it, are there
    flowers on it?—
Of the fresh grave of Koloman Wallisch,
Of the barred window—but are there flowers on it, are
    there flowers on it?—
Of his wife Paula in an Austrian prison.

The young voices rise, knowing neither of what they sing
Nor of the living and the dead for whom they sing,
United, united through time, chains, space.
And when they announce the landing on distant riverbanks
Of the bright boats of Stepan the Brigand,
The liberator,
The hero, the executioner, the executioner of executioners,
The herald,
I see, growing upon the shimmering ripples of the water,

The invigorating specter
Of a barbarous freedom drunk on its own sobs.

Stenka was broken alive on the wheel on the sixth of June,
	sixteen seventy,
Opposite the Kremlin,
In front of the church of Saint Basil the Blessed
And the Tower of the Savior.

As they break his bones, Stenka yells at his cowardly
	brother, who is lamenting his fate:
Shut up, dog!
These are his last words, his proud words, his only words
	under the ax,
They burst through the searing pain of his hacked-off limbs,
His right arm, his left leg,
They flow from his lips, mixed with bloody saliva,
A crowd collects them amid the disgusting stench
Stagnating below the scaffold.
History will preserve them like the words of Christ.

But dogs are not cowardly animals,
Dogs maintain their canine dignity very well
In this bitch of a life
And yet for centuries we have trained them in our own
	image.

My cowardly brother, shut up!
Before the torment of one who, stronger than you, better
	than you,
Dying for you, dies more than you.

Orenburg, July [19]34.

III. *Confessions*

We were never what we are,
these faces of our lives are not our own,
these voices you hear, these voices that spoke so loudly
    through the storm,
these voices are not our own,
nothing you saw is true,
nothing we did is true,
we are wholly other.

We never thought our thoughts,
believed our faith,
willed our will,
today our only truth is despair,
this confession of an insane degeneration,
this fall into darkness
where faith is denied and regained one last time.

We have neither faces nor names, neither strength nor past
—for everything is obsolete.
We should never have existed
—for everything is devastated.
And it is we who are the guilty, we the unforgivable, we the
    most wretched, we the most damaged, we are the ones,
    we are the ones, take heed
—and be redeemed!

Believe our confessions, join in our vow
of complete obedience; scorn our disavowals.
Once extinguished, the old revolt is mere obedience.

Let others less devoted be proud,
let others who have forgiven themselves be proud,
let others more devoted be proud,
let others who have not given in be proud.

If we roused the peoples and made the earth of continents
    shake,
shot the powerful, destroyed the old armies, the old cities,
    the old ideas,
began to redo everything with these defiled old stones,
    these tired hands, and what little soul we had left,
it is not in order to haggle with you now,
sad revolution, our mother, our child, our flesh,
our decapitated dawn, our night with its stars askew,
with its inexplicable Milky Way torn asunder.

If you betray yourself, how can we not betray ourselves with
    you?
After lives like these what death is possible if not, in this
    betrayal, a death for you?

What else could we have done than kneel before you
in this shame and this anguish,
if in serving you we called down on you such darkness?

If others find in your heart stabbed a thousand times over
something to live on and resist you in order to save you in
    twenty years,
a hundred years,
we who never believed in benediction bless them,
we who can do no more bless them
in our heart of hearts.

We belong no more to the future, we belong entirely to this
    age:
it is bloody and vile in its love of mankind,
we are bloody and vile like the people of this age.

Trample on us, insult us, shower us in spittle,
loathe us,
massacre us,

our love is greater than this humiliation,
this suffering,
this massacre,
your iniquitous mouths are just, your mouths are our
    mouths,
we are in you,
your bullets are our bullets, our mortal agony, our death,
    our infamy are yours,
and your vast life on these fields tilled for centuries is
    forever ours!

Paris, 12 October [19]38.

Boat on the Ural

Five men, plus one woman—
six in one boat.
Guess which is the deaf one, which the blind one,
the lost one, the frantic one,
the one who is mad for silence,
and the one whose soul dances
more lightly than suffering,
presences and absences,
smiles in the depths of the water,
prison bars on the pale sky . . .

Men sing to beguile their darkness
when they are drunk.
We are assuredly men
and more lucid than even the drunkest.
Let us sing, too. *Volga, Volga,*
here they come,
the tall bright boats of Stenka . . .

The riverbank slowly oscillates
—red rocks, the steppe, the woods—
what is weeping in our voices,
what is groaning,
what is singing in our hearts?

> *Arise, proletarians of the world!*
> *Heave! Ho!*
> *the boatmen pull the rope,*

the rope around the neck.
Sing, Alexis, your number's up,
old insurgent,
with that coolie's mug,
life's not so easy.

Row, Vassily, row, let's all
row together, we are brothers
in defeat and hard times—
our defeat is prouder and greater
than their lying victory . . .
Rowing upstream is fine
as long as our backs can take it . . .
We'll hold on as long as we can.

    Kiss the girl you fancy . . .

Jacques purses his thin lips a little
like a wise Jew who will grow old.
Boris with the profile of a hungry wolf
drinks in the sadness of an evening without drink.
No one doubts you, my friend,
if you are lost, what can we do?

    Our time is short,
    fill my glass . . .

Whether Gypsy or Egyptian
she grasps at pleasure as it slips away
(where are thesis, antithesis,
where is love, the divine synthesis?)
and dips her hands in the water
—against the current.

Yesterday, twenty-six and eleven fell
from heaven to a brilliant death.
Deaths of others, how light you are!
Joys of others, how bitter you are!

Where are the troubled waters,
troubled like you?

Softly the chorus begins again—
—no! full-throated in this empty evening,
this evening without struggle and without hope,
full-throated one last time:

> If the wind raises barricades,
> if the paving stones flash like lightning,
> before the people, comrades . . .

Night falls, the boat pulls in,
stop singing.
Exile relights its captive lamps
on the shore of time.

Oh solitudes, here we are,
upright and free and willing,
faithful to what people are making
of these times.

Orenburg, 20 May [19]35.
(About a boat trip that we six deported Communists took.)

Tête-à-Tête

Sane as I am, there are moments when I feel I'm going mad,
my psychiatry manual has nothing to say about that, the
    specialists
would say: "It's strange, but you do seem normal, those are
    just ideas,
get some rest, my friend, get some rest,
and before you go to sleep at night, whisper 'everything is
    OK, everything is OK'
thirty-three times"—
and when these specialists spoke to me in such an amicable
    way,
pity would rush in like the tide,
for I know they are mad.

Sane as I am, only the nutcases would welcome me like
    brothers
with their definitive laughter
bursting out at the beginning of the world.

You whom they welcomed, a specter of yourself,
I see your face change as if at the memory of a crime,
lit from below by an inexpiable light,
my lover, my enemy, enemy to yourself,
but you are the victim and your hatred your punishment.

My eyes are stones in sockets of flesh,
and these stones hurt you,
these stones wound you,
for you think my eyes strip you and judge you,
but it is you who judge me, my poor pitiless love,
and I who am stripped bare.

I feel storm and rage rising within you, no one can say

whence it comes, how it erupts, exceeding the boundaries of
    the human,
inhuman,
this demented tempest where you are no more than an
    ardent shadow,
where I am but a mask—a mask on a gravestone.

Time weighs less heavily than a ravaged mask.

And when your features grow calm and brighten, oh alive
    all the same!
you say: "Ah, I would just like some peace . . ." and in that
    great word *peace* there are already
slack waves at dawn under new leaves,
innocent leaves,
a welcome, a presence, a fulfillment,
there is what is not, what will *never* be.
(We know it so well, you and I, everything is there:
my strength forever strained to the point of death,
your defeat forever feeding on itself.)

They are quite wrong to say mad people's ideas are not
    reasonable,
because they outstrip our commonplace reasons for doing
    absurd things,
our petty reasons for blindness, dullness, gratification,
our unreasonable reasons for escaping genuine anguish.

Old Sigmund Freud explains it in his delirium:
The Oedipus complex has a Gorgon's head.
Old Skardanelli answers old Sigmund:
"On the splendor of man depends the splendor of life."

O[renburg], 1935.

Note. – Near the end of his life, Hölderlin, a schizophrenic, signed the
name Skardanelli to poems antedated by a century.

Dialectic

I.

We were born
in the time of the first perfected machine guns;
They were waiting for us, those excellent perforators
of steel armor plating and brains haunted by spirituality . . .

Make no mistake, ever since we began to ply the trade
of most unwilling victim
—almost since the beginning of time—
we have known how to drink every bitter cup,
gall, hemlock—very much out of style—the guillotined
    man's little glass of rum . . .

Jamaica rum, the sap of life of the tropics,
be sweet on the palate of the ashen-faced fellow who's
    paying for other people's crimes
and ours,
and drop into our mouths a little of the bitterness
his mouth distills for the peace of better men.

We know how to bear all the crosses, wooden crosses,
    swastikas,
climbing a little Calvary is really not such a big deal
for the thieves and Christs the whole lot of us are.
We have guts.
Ecce Homo proletarians
and ever-serviceable intellectuals.

And if we must end up again with our backs to the wall of
    the desperate Communards
—that is where we will be!

No doubt somewhat despite ourselves, once the wine is
      poured, we'll drink it.
Long live the Commune, hail world, long live man!
Cream of assassins, brass hats, hey, Versaillais!
Watch out, Signor Capitan, for the last step
in the last cellar:
my check is cashed at the Cheka.

II.

These are leaders of armies, big bourgeois, great
      executioners?
Heroes of the battles of Polesye, Volhynia, the Carpathians?
These are generals, these trembling, stubby-legged,
      lachrymose old men
with wet eyes and muddled hearts?
These are Chevaliers-Gardes, with the Cross of Saint George,
      the Cross of Saint Andrew?
Hey, go on then, Saint Capitalist the Assassinated,
it's your turn now.
As for me, I don't give a damn if you don't know what
Monsieur le Marquis de Galliffet did,
Me neither, I know nothing about it, I'm just an overseer
      from Gorlovka,
I haven't read any books.
But there is someone greater than us who hasn't forgotten a
      thing.

III.

By order of the Rev. Comm.
they perish in a ditch in Chernavka,
under the sabers of metalworkers from Taganka, miners
      from Kashtanka,
and an anarchist bleeding from the death of his dream.

They perish exactly as did Messieurs de Montmorin,
de Sombreuil, de Rulhière, Gentlemen of the King's
    Bedchamber,
on the second of September seventeen ninety-two, at the
    Abbaye prison.
Throat-slitting makes a muffled sound, a mad,
disgusting sound,
the sound of a crowd, the wild and sinister
sound of waves.
Bailiff Maillart consulted a big register.
"To La Force!" He wiped his face with the back of his gray
    hand.
Ah, a strong hand is needed to serve the first republic!
At dusk Citizen Billaud came to harangue the killers:
"Sansculottes! Brutus, Cinna, the splendors of Rome,
the revolution will live forever and ever,
the Commune is sending you a cask of good wine."

IV.

"See," said the young, freckle-faced propagandist,
"see how materialist history repeats itself."

V.

So well have you taught us the dirty trade of the strongest
that in the end we will become passed masters at it.
We too will have ringing hearts, pulsing brows,
eyes full of images as horrible as remorse . . .
And then let them bury us and then let them forget us,
so that nothing begins again and the earth might
    flourish . . .

Let's go, let's go, let's go!

Orenburg [19]35.

Be Hard

(Fragment)

Not a single new thought comes to you, comrade,
your problem has no solution,
your problem's made of reinforced concrete, with a steel
    reinforcement bar,
and we're inside it.

Let's be hard, as hard as chains, in time the flesh will wear
    out chains,
in time the spirit will snap chains,
in time and with Bickford fuses, of course, and the
    meticulous clockwork of machines very mistakenly
    called infernal—for the others are more infernal—
we will need time, flesh, spirit, technology, we will need
    them, that is certain:

let's be hard for a long time to come.

(And you, be hard after we're gone! And pass on the
    watchword till the end of time!)

Constellation of Dead Brothers

André who was killed in Riga,
Dario who was killed in Spain,
Boris whose wounds I dressed,
Boris whose eyes I closed.

My dear camerado
David, dead without knowing why
in a sweet orchard in France—
David, your astonished suffering
—six bullets for a twenty-year-old heart . . .

Karl, whose nails I recognized
when you had already turned to earth,
you, with your brow of such lofty thought,
ah! what was death doing with you!
Tough, dark human vine.

The north, the waves, the ocean
capsize the boat, the Four, deathly pale,
drink deeply of fear,
farewell to Paris, farewell to you all,
farewell to life, God damn it!

Vassily, through our sleepless midnights
you had the soul of a fighter
from Shanghai,
and now the wind erases your grave
in the cornfields of Armavir.

Hong Kong lights up, the hour of tall buildings,
the palm tree resembles the scimitar,
the square resembles the cemetery,
it's a sweltering evening and you are dying,
Nguyen, in your prison bed.

And you, my decapitated brothers,
the lost ones, the unforgiven,
the massacred, René, Raymond,
guilty but nowise denied.

Oh rain of stars in the darkness,
constellation of dead brothers!

To you I owe my blackest silence,
my resolve, my indulgence
for all these seemingly empty days,
and whatever is left to me of pride
for a blaze in a desert.

But let silence descend
on these lofty figureheads!
The ardent voyage continues,
the course is set on good hope . . .

When is your turn, when is mine?

The course is set on good hope.

(1935.)

Max

Max,
you died
at twenty-three,
died without knowing peaceful work
or love.

Max,
you were condemned by your youth.
It weighed
on your shoulders like a cross
in the cities and in the prisons
of Europe.

Your youth condemned you
to the certain death of soldiers
—because all the human springtime
of that era had to die.
What was avenged on your
proletarian destiny
through prison, through famine,
through the vermin
that gnawed your flesh, your heart
when we were under guard back there
behind barbed wire,
penned in sordid jails back there
by obscure and doleful men,
by cowardly and sad and desolate men?

—How we died there, my brother!
With bitter hearts, hungry bellies,
lice sucking our skin, hate
making its rounds in our brains,
its old rounds,

its exasperating, fortifying
old rounds.

But you remained like a child,
purer, better, like a vaguely
triumphant child
and far away, right here, you loved
the great suffering for the great dream,
the great conquest begun
by murdered communes.

In the sea's salt breeze
hope unfurled in you
all one morning and all one evening.
That was very good and very bitter.

Then through days of riot,
through long days of hunger,
through long days of war,
you bore the sadness
and distress
of your doomed youth.

You suffered at not finding
in the sky of this poor country
the star glimpsed at sea.

(We have yet to conquer that star,
we have yet to create it ourselves
with our hands, with our lives,
with our deaths,
with your death . . .)

The city with its cold palaces
where the revolution is hungry,
with its gray people in arms,

with those girls on the streets,
and all those soldiers departing,
and all those women in tears
in the railroad stations—
the wounded city suffered in you.

And that was the sum total of your life.
And our mutilated victories
were your faith.

Max,
among the sacrificed young lives
your young life was needed, Max.

All the broken young wings,
all the slaughtered valor
are necessary to what is being born.

Max,
for the silent rising of the sap
in the branches of the young birches,
for the sprouting of the wheat,
for the future glory of ideas,
for all this ascent of mankind,
the deaths of thousands of young men
were necessary.

For the victory
of workers republics
come to rebuild the world
upon the graves,
your anonymous death,
your forsaken death,
your loveless death,
your forgotten death,

your death, Max,
was no doubt necessary
on that wretched hospital bed,
amid what mortal agonies—
through what immense shipwreck of everything
	in you?

Max,
your last look of reproach
and anxious questioning
toward the indifferent living
at the hour of reckoning when the final sweat
moistened your poor unhaloed brow
was necessary.

And you died like the others:

Forgive us for outliving you.

Petrograd, 1921.

City

Ash, granite,
ice, snow, gold,
on metal and on flesh
(crushed).

Your cathedrals are icebergs,
your estuary is an ice field.
Cold torments your granite
and your granite enchains a river.

Your river is made of crystal under a meter of snow,
but under this river, in the darkness, another river
sweeps the secret waters of the North to the ocean.

Architects designed your least features,
vast curves, right angles, colonnades,
dead city ideal for future tourists.

In your squares bronze horsemen immortalize
their ancient despotic gestures
much prized by filmmakers.

Poets lived glumly
among your vanquished population.

Engineers, despots, and poets,
your people without rights or joy nourished them,
glorified,
understood,
betrayed them,
carried them to their graves
in the purest winters
under the whitest snows.

City, city, vast city,
vast immobile city,
I know full well there are flames
devouring you beneath the snow.
In the depths of your wide-open northern skies,
in the depths of the wide-open eyes of your dead,
the steely North Star
inscribes its lofty certitude.

City, city, vast city,
golden spires, granite, domes,
sail on, sail on toward the pole.

All life under granite,
all fervor under ice.

You are no cemetery,
you are an immense vessel,
the first one bound
for the dawn or for death.

This is a voyage of no return,
city, city, it's time to set off.

Petrograd, 1920.

26 August 28

I ran through the city, I read the newspapers
and I saw people in offices;
someone lied to me, I lied right back,
we smiled,
and I was paid for the pointless wear and tear on my brain.

I took leave of a dead man. It was raining lightly
on the cheap, red wooden coffin.
Some drunks were singing.

You were still alive.

We must be strong, we must be hard,
we must go on,
I will go on,
but really, that's hard.

And always having to understand!

Enter my eyes, peace of a summer evening,
I need it badly.
—The train stopped and it was night
and it was midnight.

Detskoye Selo, leaves at the windows,
the house asleep,
these two breaths mingling,
electric light,

this absurd sorrow that had to be shaken off,
nerves, fatigue, we let ourselves go.

And it was over, some lines written,
it was midnight, it was one o'clock

—I will go on—
the hour of your death.

Brother and comrade, they killed you last night,
at this very hour.

The transparent night caressed the steppe,
stars rained down on the cornfields.
Enormous black wounds in the sky frightened you.

Kurgannya Road,
Armavir District,
Kuban Region,
red wheat land,
26 August 28.

Farewell, everything is ending, world, brothers, plains,
eyes,
snow, cities, stars,
International,
farewell, it's crazy, why, why,
we are men,
I don't want to—

Immense fear.
Sawed-off rifle, dumdum bullet,
pierced heart,
smashed forehead, the rifle butt is heavy,
death is light.
Silence.

Brother, your thoughts vanished
through the black wound of the sky.

26–30 August [19]28.

Death of Panait

Finished—the Mediterranean, finished Paris, finished,
    finished,
finished, that corner of Alexandria where you almost died
    of hunger,
of cholera,
of despair
—does anyone know what he dies of?

Finished—the romances, dark lips and golden eyes
in the back of some dive, in the ports,
in the depths of the night.

Finished—the bitter,
intoxicating
temptations of the sea.
The *Andros* is underway for Piraeus,
the *Santa Mercedes* for Brindisi, the Indies,
Insulindia,
but you remain, eager and sad and penniless on the edge of
    a hotel bed where dark braids drift
across breasts whose moonlight your hands caress . . .
You chew yourself out and you love her, it's stupid, your
    poem,
Angelica, Genevieve, you sweet, sweet little whore . . .

Finished—the women, the innocent, the consenting, the
    repentant, the betrayed, the abandoned,
the forgiven,
and the most purely loved! —So desirable, those maids
at the Salt Lake Inn . . .

Finished—the paprika dishes and that slightly rough red
    wine
shared with rogues as you swapped stories . . .

But maybe they were good men,
and maybe they were saints,
your pals
in the little café in Brăila
where tough customers
smuggled contraband
at the Paradise.

"Not one, you see, not one of them
would've left the other in the lurch.
They weren't writers."

Finished—the books you admire
the way a child admires the marvelous
little stones
found at the seashore,
thrown up from the seafloor . . .

Finished—the books you write . . .
Good Lord, the copies! People who haven't done it don't
    know what's involved
and how fed up you can get!

The pages sold, the pages lost, truth, falsehood,
this pile of big and little lies, all those words
that are traps, junk, trickery—
and the celebrity!
The sad pages you are ashamed of having written,
and those you could not extract from your brain . . .
The tiring, discouraging, exhausting pages that suddenly
    come to life
where Nerrantsoula struts, more beautiful and proud of
    herself and happier to be alive than in real life
—where Nerrantsoula walks off, swinging her hips, and
    dives into the Danube under the open sky,
oh pale swimmer, in love with the water . . .

The heart of hearts of men that you spit out in your work.
Is all that printed paper at Rieder's
still selling?

Finished—the insults,
They spared you none.
They got fat stuffing them down your throat until your
    death, and even after.
So
thanks to you a lot of people ate better than you did.
They said you were a traitor, that you sold out, my poor
    friend!
You, the faithful one, betraying all those phrasemongers,
you, a sellout, who had nothing to sell, and yourself
    unsalable!
You lay upon your press clippings, like Job upon his filth,
gently spitting up the last remnant of your lungs
into the faces of the hacks,
the glorifiers of profitable massacres,
the profiteers of disfigured revolutions . . .

Finished—even the wish to die
when only bastards are left in this vale of promotional tears.
For you botched it earlier because you loved the earth too
    much.
You were left with a scar across the carotid
and your suicide attempt made it hard to wear detachable
    collars.

Your last unfinished pages pull away from you
like a flight of doves,
darkness and ashes, return to darkness, return to ashes—
you'd like to cry, but that's not possible, oh sure, cry, you
    must be joking!

You stumble, the road's burning stones slip from under
    your feet,
"hold me up, gracious friends!" —Hold him up, gracious
    friends, hold him up,
the sky is blinding, ah, what heartbreak!
You go off between two goddesses, they reassure you, they
    lead you away,
consoling you:
solitude, friendship.

No more will I see you going from room to room
stirring your black mood
into your cup of black coffee.
No more will I calm your vehement rages.
No more will I see your veiny Balkan hands,
your big, gold-filled mouth,
your hunter's nose, your eyes of a sly old child,
a cynic among the cunning . . .
And we won't go to Provence with packs on our backs and
    taking pictures
as if we were twenty,
no charge for the beautiful girl and the madman, the bride-
    to-be and the anarchist . . .
Those were the days.

I have sighed over you so often at night
that this evening, in this desert, I feel close to you,
closer than to the living.
The same winds blow across my steppe and your Baragan,
the same storms . . .
The Great Bear sparkles in my window; and behind the
    house stretches the plain, so vast and barren it seems
    like the end of the world,
a young woman is asleep here, exhausted from work, calm
    in her giving.

The fresh sadness of your death torments me and soothes
     me.
All this is your gravestone and it will be mine and it is
     already ours,
our continued life.

I am listening in your stead
to such a radiant silence falling upon the clamor.

O[renburg], [19]35.

Why Inscribe a Name?

In the Koktebel cemetery in the Blue Mountains,
the Tartars put only a stone on their graves,
not even cut, with no inscription.

Why inscribe a name when the man is no more?
For us? Then, they ask, do you believe that we could forget
    him?
For God? But God has known him for all eternity.

These wise people thus know nothing of the administration
and its profitable little traffic in thirty-year concessions
or of the bourgeois pleasure of buying oneself a
    monumental vault
more expensive
than a poor person's fate or a proletarian's house.

Cassiopeia

You told me, Oxana, that he died this morning
despite you,
despite your youth, despite your grace, your pity, your hands,
your care,
you told me of your distress at the death of this stranger,
nameless, ageless, faceless,
who from a distance resembled Christ on the torture tree,
    but more naked,
who for years sipped from his cup between temperature
    charts and banishment orders.
"Ah, if only I could have tried those last injections," you
    were saying,
"but I didn't come on duty till eleven o'clock,
his heart had already failed,
I only found him at the morgue, with his fine features."

The names of diseases, Oxana, are words
we throw at the ailments, wounds, deaths at work inside us.
That relentless old organ the heart gets carried away, plays
    sly tricks, gets abused,
what could your little vials and aseptic needles do
when the whole exhausted planet was collapsing in there?

Tracked down, this dead man I never saw
is with us, now that he no longer exists, he has followed us
    through this holiday.
And when I put my hand on Tatiana's shoulder, the Other
    who is inside me, who is bigger and better than I, and
    who knows the secret, said to the dead man so near:
This hand belongs to you, and I give you this shoulder.

Young woman, you must give him your shoulder—let
    him lean on it—you must give him everything, you
    understand: he is dead,

now he has only our warmth, now he has only my arms to
	embrace you,
and no one else in the world but you, since I am the only
	one who knows.

The bands have passed, the rather grotesque floats have
	passed,
the flags, the processions, the soldiers
singing of towns taken on the shores of the Pacific,
the athletes have passed, the blue clouds that caressed the
	steppe have passed.
There was a barefoot little Mongol shepherd in a felt hat
	who merrily followed the snapping flags like a praise
	singer's musician,
he has gone past,
you remain.

The day has passed, with its clamor, its blaring brass bands,
	its radiant sun,
all alone with you, I am given this shoulder, this naked
	breast, this consenting mouth, this forgiven soul, close
	to me, close to you
and all your past warmth is inside me.

My dead stranger, have I not misjudged, despised, insulted
	you in our separate lives,
our helpless lives,
now,
you, frozen, under the earth, and us, upright upon the
	earth, nothing separates us anymore, reunited as we are
by the risen stars and this sign between us: the high
	glittering triangles of Cassiopeia.

O[renburg], Summer [19]35.

Song

Destins, destins impénétrables . . .
        —Apollinaire

Destinies impenetrable destinies
cities are built on sand
but the deserts will bloom again
oh heart of the inexhaustible world
hope refuses to perish

this hard will my precious delirium
suffering you must smile suffering
whether the wound bleeds or cries out
the gods have nothing more to tell you
the jungle is your only home

the earth has the eyes of panthers
do you truly feel love for the earth
sky rent by comets
absurd child in despair
are you the victim of poets

archer who keeps watch and forgives
oh you who never give up
welcome this shade born for you
does she not surrender all her pride
to every passerby sent by you

the archer succumbs the stone splits
the flower is a cry of triumph
do you want us to be brothers
I bring a glimmer into this void
nothing will tarnish this spark

Imagine if you found peace again
that slack water beneath the palms
flesh is in need of the knife
have you betrayed the dawn of peace
night devours the torches

let a solitary blaze remain to me
I am standing nothing else will die
totter oh Cordillera of the Andes
Elbrus pure snows of fervor
join your ardent heights

divine spinning planet
your Eurasias your singing seas
the simple scorn for executioners
and here we are merciful thought
almost like heroes

Trust

I have seen the steppe turn green and the child grow up,
My eyes meet the human gaze
of Toby, a good dog who trusts me.

Azure touches the earth, we breathe in the sky.
Red cows graze under glorious clouds,
and from afar the slender Kirghiz girl who tends them
seems delivered from all misery.

Setting sun, behold our hearts, take them!
Behold our bodies which you fill with radiance,
Behold us washed,
purified,
liberated,
pacified
at the point where river, plain, and sky meet.

Nothing is forgotten, nothing is lost, we are
true,
truly men, men true to men
regardless of the moment, the risk, the burden, the
    punishment,
the hatred,
true and trusting.

My son, my grown son, we are going to cleave the water
with slow strokes.
Let's trust in the river pierced by sunbeams,
trust in these waters drunk by our brothers, the drowned.

Trust in the frail, supple muscles of the child
who dives from the steep bank, then cries out:
"Oh Father, it's terrible and good, I'm touching bottom,
Daylight is mixed with darkness, and it's shivery, shivery . . ."

Grace of the slender body darting through the air, through
    the water,
trust with eyes closed, trust with eyes open.

What more perfect parabolas than in the flight of birds?
My thought follows it, just as quick, just as sure,
an arrow through the nonextended,
laden with moving images by all that has been,
ethereal and prodigal,
offering the unique future many a possible future.

The beetle rests on the wild rose,
our shadows have scared off the tadpoles in the pond,
it is a magnificent, peaceful day and the earth rolls on,
sweeping along day, night, dawns, evenings,
tropics, poles, deserts,
cities
and our thoughts,
our shared journey through the infinite,
the eternal,
and our eyes,
toward the constellation of Hercules, itself swept along
by such floods of stars that all darkness vanishes
—defeat swept away . . .

O[renburg], [19]34.

Sensation

For L ...
("Don't be sad . . .")

After that splendid Notre Dame inverted
in a Seine pure of the clochards' remorse,
after that trembling rose window abloom in the dark water
where the stars spin out their inconceivable threads
across profiles of sea horses and foliage as real as mirages,

what remains, oh my madly reasonable spirit,

what still remains inaccessible to the wide-awake sleeper
who follows down these dark quays, from one Commune to
    the next,
the hope-filled cortege of his executed brothers?

Paris, [19]38.

II. Messages

In Paris, in December 1938, I published a collection of poems called *Resistance*, which was dedicated to my brothers and comrades in Russia, without my knowing whether they were alive or dead.

I did not foresee the fortunes of this word and that mankind's Resistance to the powers of annihilation would become the essential spiritual fact of our times. I used these lines from Péguy as the epigraph:

> Another will smash the prison register.
> Another will smash the doors of the jail.
> Another will wipe from our thin shoulders
> The dust and blood fallen from our necks.

Let them also accompany the messages of this new collection, which I dedicate in loyalty to my surviving friends and comrades from the black years and to our dead, too numerous to name . . .

V. S., Mexico City, April [19]46.

Sunday

The singer was singing oh life is so beautiful
The singer was not at all beautiful
She couldn't shut up she couldn't go away
She was singing oh it's so beautiful

A corpse in a fedora was staggering in the revolving door
With his calamitous overcoat he dared not enter this
    overpriced café
In that greenhouse heat what would have become of him
    just up from underground
He might have lost his lower jaw his teeth the blue marbles
    of his eyes
They might have rolled under the banquette among the
    cigarette butts
So waiter pick up the gentleman's eyes don't be afraid they
    won't burn you

People took him for a pauper still among the living since he
    knew how to say excuse me madam thank you sir when
    they put fifty centimes in the palm of his decomposed
    hand
And then he was lucky not to look like a dirty Jew
As for me I felt at a certain point on the back of my neck
A small blue terrifically radiant pain
Comparable I think to the pain felt by people shot so
    expertly they hardly suffer
But more long-lasting
Because I kept hearing the singer oh life is so beautiful

And the customers the waiters the singer the corpse in the
    fedora we all got along famously

With the exhausted horsemen of an Apocalypse completely
    devoid of interest
Who trotted along with their why-not in the dark lowering
    sky of Boulevard Rochechouart.

March [19]39.

Bérangère

The prisoner was a charming girl
Oh radiant Bérangère
Be glad be glad my lovely child
These keys aren't heavy tonight

She was but twenty years old
At midnight in her cell
We loved we loved so very much
I wept the morning she died

I was for her she was for me
She loved like nobody else
You know I have a tender heart
And hanging's an awful shame

The prisoner is in hell tonight
An angel weeps alone
Your flowing tears my lying mouth
And our eternal chains

There's not a boat that does not sink
Three hundred fathoms deep
The sky above is none too bright
Not even if money don't stink

Suicide of Dr. C.

Pure northern night on the steppe, pure solitude of
    northern snow
With my lost manuscripts, with a devastated shade, with
    our fraternal perils,
My son had just gone to sleep, it was warm in the house of
    clay and tree trunks built at the very edge of the void, by
    unknown hands, for us and that unique moment,
You came in, doctor. You came from beyond the comets that
    rend the skies,
You, whiter than snow under the stars, you, icier than that
    December night on the Ural plain,
You, more silent than the night, more absolute, more at
    peace, more nocturnal.

Doctor, don't say a word, everything has been said, you
    killed yourself the other night in Paris,
That is much truer than your psychiatric work.
Welcome. You are proof that words are not possible
    anymore.
It was an amazing Paris night, a night with the universe
    splendidly whirling about,
You understood everything so well there was really nothing
    more to understand,
Nothing more to wait for,
You were so alone with that nameless relief that it was like
    the exaltation of an immense love just like the midnight
    sun on the ice floes.
You looked at your collections, distractedly, collections,
    books, what an idea!
Portraits, why portraits when the planet is empty?
You went through the rooms, smoking, calm calm calm
—with a great song in your breast, a song you did not hear,
    a song of definitive silence,
in the mirrors you saw the necessary visage of your farewell,

Calm calm calm calm farewell
—you cocked the pistol, I can see your last distraught smile,
    calm calm calm farewell—the pistol,
It was no longer Paris, it was the pole, no, it was no longer
    this strange universe, admirable and cruel,
But perhaps galaxy M101 in Ursa Major
Or the one in Andromeda?
The axis of the worlds wobbled slightly beneath your
    footsteps.

There's no point in living, doctor, no point in living once
    the miracle is over.
It was no longer worth being the lucid madman who cured
    other madmen.
Calm calm calm farewell—the pistol.

Orenburg–Ural, 1934.

Marseille

Planet without visas, without money, without compass,
    great empty sky without comets,
The Son of Man has nowhere left to lay his head,
His head a target for mechanical shooters,
His Remington portable and his last suitcase
Bearing the names of fifteen fallen cities . . .

> *Moscou   Vienne   Berlin*
>   *Barcelone, Barcelone!*
> *Paris Parc Montsouris*
> *Orléans, Beaugency, Notre-Dame de Cléry,*
>   *Vendôme, Vendôme!*

What is to be done if the horizon looks so much like a
    prison?
All the exiles in the world are at the Greek informer's café
    tonight,
Indecisive suicides stroll along the quay, looking at
Chaloupes called *Désir, Île de Beauté,*
    Notre-Dame-de-la-Garde,
They're afraid of roundups as suicides out for a walk never
    have their papers in order.
They say they should write to the American Committee,
They read the newspapers, they laugh, they smoke, they
    almost pass for proper living persons,
"We have to laugh, madam, at this mad enterprise, the
    universal extinction of the Jews,
You won't get anywhere, there are too many of them, and
    then the Rich will always save themselves, they will say:
    'We're Aryans.'
People will believe them because they pay,
And the poor, madam, whether Jews or Aryans, are nothing."

The Son of Man listens, he drinks a *menthe*, he remembers
    he is flat broke,
But he doesn't give a damn,
the main thing tonight would be to draft the seventh thesis
    on permanent revolution.

His notepad is full of dazzling ideas ready to explode in
    flashes,
But they had to be encoded in conventional terms that no
    one will understand when he is gone

He sets off for the transporter bridge, gazing at the absurdly
    peaceful sky,
Absurdly, he suddenly feels as peaceful as this sky,
He is glad to be alive thanks to the big seagulls flying over
    the harbor
And perhaps he would be just as glad to die at this moment
The death of a militant, metallic and violent, almost
    expected,
But these are things one would rather feign not to know,
Things one half admits to oneself and then only with
    disapproval.

Some idle prostitutes behind the windows of a sleazy little
    bar
Say: He must be a Russian or a Jew or some Spanish
    anarchist,
Sure are a lot of these foreigners on their uppers these days,
    I can't wait till they pack them off to Africa!
Under a dark halo, some misshapen bargemen play with
    limp cards,
Trumps, I pass, clubs,
Big Jules is explaining the clever vermicelli racket,
Jupiter and Saturn shine high in the sky.

Marseille, 1941.

The rats are leaving . . .

The rats are leaving the sinking freighter because rats are
    little gray gnawing rodents,
Rats fear the sea and death, rats care only about themselves,
The rats will drown all the same, but the plague they carry
    will live on
In other rats, fat gray rats, rich treacherous rats that think
    they're great conquerors.

Neither purifying storms nor salutary torpedoes nor
    scientific disinfections can do a thing about it.

See, even the plague can't drive us to despair.

We must not leave this great liner that is going to founder,
    we must stay on board
For the last handshake and the last swig of wine
Among emigrants with tenacious hearts gone forever to
    other continents.
We are neither the first nor the last, we simply form a
    human chain
From one misfortune to the next effort and from one
    shipwreck to the next dawn.
We must not leave the great defeated worlds, we must hold
    on to them with a bitter grip
As one clings to floating hulks.

And so may singing hulks carry us off with the bracing
    memory of the drowned,
May they lull our thirst slaked by salt water through
    demented nights,
Those among us who hold on, the toughest, guided by the
    North Star and the Southern Cross,
Will drink one day from gently delirious waters.

And we will arrive, my steadfast traveling companions!
On a morning of amber, crystal, and snow, in a torrid calm,
We will have unforgiving faces, hands turned absolutely
    inexorable,
Such a fearsome knowledge of justice,
We will feel welling up in our breasts a joy so ravaged by
    silence and suffering
That we will start life anew with strictly necessary
    massacres.

Martinique, [19]41.

Out at Sea

For L.

The Cuban artist with the handsome Negroid profile struck
    in China,
across the ages,
Is drawing metallic saw-toothed monsters:
He knows we're all lost if we don't smash the teeth of the
    machines.

In the brisk air of departure I am waiting for Marseille, that
    court of miracles of defeated revolutions, to vanish
    below the horizon,
Its Old Port decked out in destitution, its cafés, its crowds,
Its godless basilica erected on the golden rock.

I am thinking of you. You're passing by the Brûleur de
    Loups, you're alone, you bear our solemn love,
It is a burning, it is a wound, it is flowing water, it is our
    thirst-quenching spring in the desert,
You are sure, you are pure, you are my thirst-quenching
    spring out at sea.
You are walking down Rue Pavillon with a determined step
    signaling ardor, anxiety, timidity, pride,
You are pretty, you know it, you are devoted, you do not
    know what you are, in a little while you will doubt
    yourself and the world
In the panic of twilight, heartbreak, forsakenness,
You will step down from the tram at the Parette stop
    and tears will fill your eyes when you recognize our
    constellations, but is that possible, is that possible?
A devastated, boundless joy will calm you. Sleep now.
I am waiting to see shining in the sky, in your footprints, the
    daylight stars,

Will they be black, will they be the pupils of your eyes, will
    they be pure fire,
We will know tomorrow,
I await them in your stead, I am sure they will appear, if we
    had no confirmed miracles
We would have no recourse but to blow up the last ships or
    hang ourselves down in the hold.

I love you so simply that it's like this sea,
Obvious and radiant.
Here are the distant snows of the Pyrenees, the plain of
    Figueres,
Peaceful yet gorged with the dead who are our brothers. I
    give you this sea, this snow, this verdant plain,
Having only my eyes to see for yours.

Before the vast landscape of Castelldefels I think of you
As a comrade points out the fortifications on the Catalan
    earth in the distance,
This was a torture site for the International Brigades, he
    says,
We pass by without shame or remorse. Hail, innocent earth!
Let our innocent hands, which will be strong hands, salute
    you.

I was thanking you for living in these times and
    retempering my strength with your strength
Like that of gently powerful plants.
Night was falling over the heights along the Ebro where a
    vast fire reddened the peaks.
The sierra was bleeding fire, close to you I felt like the
    twenty-year-old fighter I once was.

Can it be that I am already fifty—with this all-consuming
    black gold in my veins, this gold for you, this gold for
    life?

My past lives, torn to shreds, snap behind me in the trade
    winds
Like tattered flags.

It's the boat that's in motion, but it's the stars that pitch
    across the sky,
I was truly expecting to experience their prodigious rocking,
I surrender to it as if to the depths of your eyes.

We are crossing the tropic in the total calm of
    accomplishment.
Perfect night. You are as real as this night. Six thousand
    meters of ocean carry us through the absolute.
Bottomless calm, nameless pride, humility. I love you.

Atlantic, April [19]41.

Caribbean Sea

Off these hot islands, these forgotten islands, caravels one
    day emerged from the sea,
The night stars were spearheads, balmy winds were blowing
    from the gates of hell,
To this forgotten world, the ships brought the Cross, they
    brought faith,
They brought strange, savage illnesses,
They brought men of savage energy,
Ruthless men from Europe and from Asia.

On this earth they knew only crucifixion,
They looked only for gold, oh Lord! to make into machines
    when they were all dead.

They were white men like centaurs, they were black men
    conquered by centaurs.
And so strong was their hope they brought mastiffs to hunt
    down hopeless men in the bush.
The Caribs had only a little mild poison on their
    arrowheads,
A little venomous cunning in their keen eyes.
Their women learned to love according to European rites,
The Caribs died as the forest dies when the land breakers
    arrive.

Mar del Caribe, voracious sea, dangerous sea, you still sing
    your menacing song for all those dead men,
You are no different with these infant lands, with today's
    little flags,
The surge of your low waves toward these lush lands is like
    a surge of hatred,
The palm trees that contemplate you without seeing you are
    shredded by it.

You are the burning, you are the storm, you are the endless
    calm violence, you are the power, you are—
But what has been slain?

Races, bodies, sweat, blood were mixed together
In muggy, fermented jungles,
With a torrid determination,
And the bellies, bellies, bellies gave birth to people of every
    human color
For every suffering, however inhuman,
For every imaginable travail,
For every imaginable murder—but that is no longer important,
Because all these faces from Eurasia, Eurafrica, Euramerica,
    and Polynesia,
Those from unknown lands, those with the most naked
    expectations,
Fine white faces, golden faces, black or copper faces, faces of
    unexpected hues
Are present today, with the hundred thousand smiles of young
    girls in pink on a night full of annoying radio music.

Danger, danger in the air we breathe, you are not the worst,
Nor is being this graying man, alone before this strange sea,
Who suddenly looks for the Eiffel Tower in the unfurled
    clouds,
Or the faded onion domes, strewn with faint stars, of a little
    old Russian church surrounded by birch trees . . .

The worst has neither name nor number nor face.

To exist without you, is that even possible?

Sharks roam this mineral sea, it seems they are always hungry.

Ciudad Trujillo,
Dominican Republic, June [19]41.

Our Children

I see, closing my eyes, I see
Stars as big as terrestrial moons
Hanging above the rafts carrying our children.
The sea, bitter darkness, pitches iridescent with infant light,
It is glacial, it is vertical, it is shifting,
Perhaps it is hopeless.
Above the rafts, spindrift unfurls strange flags that wind,
    night, and stars rip apart with a quiet sovereign fury,
And our children are calm, armed with ignorance, armed
    with wisdom.
They see in the palms of their hands warm crystals sprung
    from the deep,
They hold in their hands the miracle of seeds.

A great school of patient sharks follows the rafts,
The watery eyes of sharks contemplate our children.

Mex[ico City], Sept[ember] [19]43.

Death of Jacques Mesnil

Jacques Mesnil has finished his long, long life
Under his old capes and his corduroy suit
He died on the roads during the fall of France, in a convent,
    I don't know where.

His emaciated face bore the marks of a great, dogged
    courage,
His thin chest like that of an old saint wasted by mundane
    torments
Retained the still-warm ashes of the most exalted earthly
    blazes.

When I met him as he descended with his sprightly step on
    his way down
Toward the Pré-Saint-Gervais,
I would see his failing tenacious passion for living out in
    front, courageously,
Like a figurehead, pathetic and
Abandoned.
No more spindrift to cleave, no more dawns to surprise, no
    more future to seize on distant shores!
He also resembled those El Greco figures who suddenly
    look at you with intolerably serious eyes.

Jacques, was it you, really you, the barely aging man I met
    in Moscow,
The man who held Clara by the hand, Clara like a figure out
    of Botticelli but living, loving, thinking?
Is it really you, Jacques, who so loved age-old Florence?
—who plumbed the soul of revolutions, who heard Trotsky
    in the year nineteen twenty, during the terror,
who scrupulously strove to distinguish, amid the blood we
    were shedding, rectitude from error?

I know how lucid and firm you are, and your almost secret
      greatness.
I see you descending alone in a convulsive solitude.
No one can join you there anymore.
You are listening to the distant chords of great, perhaps
      eternal symphonies diminishing inside you
—no one will ever again listen to them with you—
And soon you won't hear them anymore. Doesn't this
      thought bring some relief?
So it was that Beethoven gone deaf heard the terrifying
      music of the spheres
And a joy greater than the darkness burst forth inside him.
I can't speak to you anymore for I see you're too close to the
      inconceivable frontier
Where words have no more meaning, where every reality is
      flickering and fading out
Like the constellations in the pale light of dawn.

I see you calmly looking off in that direction, your one eye
      filled with the last gleam of distress
I feel an urge to flee from you because I still drink my
      portion of human joy from incomparable lips,
Yet you would say to me: It's OK, Serge, everyone's got to
      live!—but you yourself are too far from carnal lights.
We have nothing more than sad handshakes at the curb to
      connect us,
They will just have to do.

How could I halt what tears through you with no end
      possible save the end of the universe?
How could I halt what so swiftly despoils you, leaving only
      an exhausted mask that frightens even you?
How could I respond to your gentle nervous laughter, the
      laughter of a ghost?

Your science of the sunset's last moments is but prescience
    of the night,
A night too deep to have prescience of the day.
You will not finish your *Life of Élisée Reclus*, you would need
    ten years' work
And you have only this bleak present of a few hours.
One morning you will fall asleep over those manuscripts as
    the birds awake
—it's finished, you are sleeping, you are no more than a
    shade inside me,
I hear strange birds singing in the palm trees,
What's become of you, what will become of your
    manuscripts?

Jacques, the serene face of your death followed me through
    the streets of Marseille amid the defeated crowds,
It conjured up sudden silences in our room, but decorum
    prevented my saying they signaled your presence.
I found you on the Atlantic in the midst of implacably
    radiant expanses,
Here you are next to me at Pointe du Bout, in the muggy
    tropical rain,
Is it my gaze or yours that follows the flight of the black
    dragonflies?

Martinique, April [19]41.

Altagracia

Oh dazzling cemetery!
A multitude of crosses hallucinate it in white,
Standing in closed ranks like living beings through a final
     discipline
Of cement and fire.

In darkest night, I saw it streaming with light.
Its battalion of crosses seemed to start moving.
A host of eyeless faces were revealed in the slanting mirrors
     of lightning bolts,
All the world's mirrors were breaking at once, sweeping
     away the disfigured faces of armies . . .
Light, light, rise up! Pure and lucid light under the rain of
     spearheads, under streams of swords;
The jungle was being torn apart by thunderous fevers,
torrents were blasting painfully exalted gravestones.

And these disfigured faces were yours, were ours
—what would I be without you, what would we be without
     them?
Black palm trees waved to us from the depths of the broken
     firmament,
then the clouds disintegrated and the stars were great fires.
Cemetery petrified by light! Torrid daylight turns it back to
     cement,
Returns it to the stupor, the blindness of the living.

I see the gravestone of Porfirio Kepi. I see a Chinese
     merchant's gravestone, which looks like his cash register,
Add up the hours, add up the lightning bolts, add up the
     glimmerings of consciousness, add up the piasters,
Deduct laughter and anxiety,
But how much do they weigh, the anxiety and the cement
     and the cherished calm lost landscapes of Hainan?

A black woman in mourning comes there early every day,
    she is skinny, she is poor, she is dressed like someone
    who would feel ashamed of not having a little money
She brings flowers, she would be ashamed of coming
    empty-handed to this emptiness,
No spark of life remains in her, she makes her way, a black
    ant,
She respectably makes her way.

I see her talking to someone in this absurd desert, she asks:
"Do you think these flowers look good here? Do you like
    them?"
She tells him the price of rice, the price of asphodels,
As she used to say, "Do you want a little more rice or coffee?"
The sun at its zenith envelops her in incandescent solitude.

What better name for her than Altagracia?
Everything must be given her in the startling vacuity of a
    name,
Like a recompense utterly vain and yet necessary,
Otherwise, complete injustice would burst upon this
    helpless being.

Ciudad Trujillo, D[ominican] R[epublic]
The cemetery, 1941.

Mexico: Idyll

In memory of Marcel Martinet

In the shade of cruel nopales the mule's eye gently glistened
Like a lover's silence
The saddle was studded with silver. The man looked like a
    black eagle
Yet he had a singing smile
He was as beautiful as the angels without fear perhaps
    without joy
With no other joy than the throbbing of the blood in his
    tense veins
He said I await thee my betrothed.

Oh sweet life oh sweet terror fresh ripe watermelon bitten
    lips
Calm vibration of the earth
Restless nights vanished beneath a thousand unknown stars
When the dark-haired girl took off her clothes.

Stones ruin her back his hands the hands of the sky bruise
    her breasts
The night full of shifting omens sizzles like a conflagration
Oh mineral coolness Imagined undulations of serpents
The very sap of lianas joins their limbs This convulsive heat
    flows from the bowels of the earth.

Oh delectable violence No murder is sweeter Lord!
Oh wrenching and submission
Death is not sweeter Lord!

Magic moon Mother moon illuminate them with your
    plainchant!

They climbed to the top of the old lava flows flesh against
    flesh on the one saddle
The tread of the mule set swaying the world the stars their
    blood their silence
Somberly pacified
The silver-trimmed harness jingled liquid stellar murmur
The smell of resin was in the air
The escort of tall black milky chandelier cacti
Surrounded them with stillness

The same bolt of lightning struck them both at the spot
    where you see a cross
(Or else it was slugs fired by people from San Juan parish—
because of the division of water from a stream)

Mexico: Morning Litany

Don't be afraid kind tourists listen

If the scientists are to be believed—when they are
    reassuring—the incubation period for leprosy is at least
    seven years
Many fellows in the flower of youth would choose this
    seven-year risk
Over flesh scorched by Flammenwerfer
In the astral glow of sulfurous bombs
They would give up a posthumously awarded Purple Heart
And splendid parades over their graves
They would cheerfully consent to their faces rotting
—hey, in seven years! seven years what an eternity of
    happiness my boy mis muchachos!
And you're going to say the true human face is noble?
For my part I have seen it in the infernal moments of which
    everyone is ignorant and I tell you it is ignoble
And that it's deserved every imaginable leprous plague
But no one deserves being burned to a crisp at the age of
    twenty
And if I talk like a man consumed with rancor forgive me
    Kind tourists listen

A las dos y a las tres
a las cuatro y a las seis
at every hour Christ the King
at every hour the Virgin Queen
at every hour drink and sorrow
at every hour a wound for me
at every hour a death for you
Holy Mother Infant Jesus
bless our land and freedom
arid land and naked man
fallen pride defeated race

the donkey licking hot stones
the serpent devoured by the eagle
and the eagle killed by vultures
the bird of fire the bird of ash
leprous blood and avidity
dead eyes and humility

"And what else my dear Mr. Jones what sort of eternity?"

Mexico: Churches

The two most Christian churches I have seen combine in
  my memory
thus two rising flames join one crimson and the other black
thus continental expanses merge the tropics and suddenly
  the pole
the jungle and suddenly the steel of glaciers inseparable in
  their inexplicable unity

One was on the Sergiyev Posad road on the way to the
  Trinity Lavra of Saint Sergius in Old Russia
on the snowy plains surrounded by sleepy woods blue and
  white
under a splendidly dazzling sun
At a bend in the road the flamboyant crimson church of
  Pushkino came into view
its tower set on the ice like a joy a joyful relief
and we were reconciled with the cold with the northern
  lights
with the polar nights
with the convulsive nights and the obsessive suns that each
  carried in his head
(We were young travelers joyfully bitter and strong on
  intimate terms with torments and death
we had real need of reconciliation with ourselves and the
  work of human hands)

After the wars revolutions mass graves inexplicable crimes
  an ocean of anxiety an ocean on the map
it was in San Juan Parangaricutiro in the state of Michoacán
  that I saw the other church the one with the black flame
volcanic ash was invading it and burying it
incandescent lava was crawling toward it through the fields
already covered with ash that was reddish and gray at once
  bright and dark

we saw molten basalt
and dark destructive snow cosmic dust cold fire dust
We seemed to see the most immense battlefields of our
    times denuded and delivered up to remorse alone
to the subdued specter of remorse alone

Little by little the church slipped into the irreconcilable
    night
a night of annihilation
cinders from the crater fumed at the end of a seedy alley
rhythmically exhaling the breath of the inhuman earth
a heavy cloud unfurled visible nothingness across the sky
tearing open blinding the Milky Way

For a few pesos some Indios gave us some ordinary
    exhausted horses of the Apocalypse
some drunken Indios had the faces of corpses that were
    delirious
yet smiling
And there were others who were very dignified they were
    eating tortillas in the halos of smoky lamps
—what calm ruled there what security in calm and certain
    destruction

And when morning came a morning as calm with
    annihilation as the night of annihilation
the Indios entered the transparently bright nave they
    entered on their knees
dragging themselves on their knees hopping on their knees
they advanced on their knees toward the altar
they stood up oddly straight before the altar
they backed out all together in an extraordinarily slow
    hopping dance
all surrounded by murmured prayers and the scuffing
    sound of their feet on the stones

men of energy and ash
reconciled with the disaster
reconciled with the death throes of the land under basaltic
    fire and ash
reconciled with the end of the world—and why not?
reconciled

Thy will be done oh Lord—oh Planet!

Carried away by the rhythm of their dance without gestures
    refusing to see us they did not see us
but we saw them we understood them deeply through a sort
    of transparence

Outbreaks

From twelve thousand meters up in the interworld the
    angel-faced aviator released
liquid-air bombs as pretty as trinkets and illustrated tracts
    full of promises and wisdom,
on the living map below he saw great white flowers shoot
    up, perfectly flawless flowers,
he was not thinking of anything for his head was equipped
    with brand-new ideas made of a metal that was
    superflexible, durable, unbreakable, and cheap.

The planet split into three, into four, into six, into six
    hundred and sixty-six parts,
six hundred and sixty-six decapitated little girls under the
    rubble of the School of Good Conduct inaugurated the
    day before by the President of the Republic.

Rescuers dug into the rubble with pickaxes,
clouds of multicolored birds suddenly flew out,
but they were headless birds that turned into bloody rags in
    the air,
into rags that turned into paper in the clouds
in the clouds that turned into mad ideas,
peaceful,
blazing,
ruthless ideas.

Père Ubu shouted: Damn it! All my chamber pots are
    broken!
Shit! Get some glue! I want a strong glue, like the Lord Our
    God ones,
that American brand, a hundred thousand tons, by air,
    cable New York and 3 percent commission,
a sacred mission!

You pack of bastards, my collection of Siamese postage
    stamps
is screwed, well, that's just how it is. I'm going to have to
    make you
a nice little revolution with mass-produced guillotines,
    standardized, electrified, et cetera
and statues of jerks in uniform on every street corner, you'll
    see!

A dictator made of polychrome glass backed his way out
    from underground,
from underground backed his way out, his buttocks
were stamped with blood-red and gold shoe prints, bigger
    than himself, it was incredible,
paper numbers were spinning in his chest,
a recording bawled from his throat: Citizens, my day of
    glory has come!
Innocent lands, wretched lands, here we are, it's really not
    our fault if that's the way we are.

Mexico City, 1941.

Philosophy

What's certain is that people have wasted a lot of time
>looking for recipes to vanquish courage,
but it's not over. Nothing is ever over, even if despair is
>playing its last card.
What's certain is that people have wasted a lot of time
>measuring the lines of force between human sorrow and
>the trajectories of comets,
but at the bottom of the sea typewriters and starfish and
>the carcasses of boys
get along famously and whatever we do
not one of us, not one child drowned before opening its
>eyes,
no matter the depth of the graves, the latitudes, the
>longitudes, the explosives, the torments, the prayers,
not one of us will fall outside this universe bounded only by
>the northern lights,
which have neither dimension nor number, neither magic
>nor duration, neither consciousness nor exchange value.
We are here for a probable eternity of rainbows alternating
>with a total darkness that a single star of the fourteenth
>magnitude inexplicably resurrects.

The wind does not die if the sail is ripped apart
and we are the vessel, the masts, the sail, the wind, the rip,
we are the bolt of lightning passing through the rip.
No algebra will demonstrate the contrary. The murdered
>sleep of bombardiers can do nothing about it.
True suicides are impossible, as the Milky Way confirms
>by its living glacial purity, which the dead will never see
>again because it resorbs them.
Besides, they no longer have a need to see, for the flame
>cannot see itself, the flame burns unaware of its own
>existence.

So stay calm and be reassured, salvation does not reside
    in fear, perhaps it lies simply in communion with fire,
    simply.
The circle of worlds has but imaginary forms, but we are as
    real as the heavens.
And if the voice that speaks this way strikes you as vain,
    forget it,
for I am only a passerby who often turns back at the
    boundary of cruel, cherished temporal certainties and
    clear eternal uncertainties.

Mexico City, Oct[ober 19]43.

We have long thought . . .

We have long thought
that the gods of our hope
would end up believing in us.
That they would shatter solitude,
disenchant the deserts
—if only in order to live.
We have been betrayed.

What are they and what are we?
A low song rises from the ashes,
The dark glow reaches its zenith
—what else remains to us?

Stars without eyes, brows
shattered by thunderstorm,
this pride at standing upright
at the edge of yawning craters,

the habit of still believing
more in the earth than in the grave,
this living desire to quell
the wild laughter bleeding in us.

—Be content with these pledges, my love,
I have none better.
I'll make them into a necklace of foam
too light to bruise you.

Mex[ico City], April [19]45.

Note

Sing me again your beautiful song:
Perhaps I will still believe it.
Whether lying or resistant,
it's the same enchantment.

Bathe in the ocean, my love,
we are too much burned by the sky.
Be perfect like the wave:
even if it hardly exists.

Someone will fall if you succumb,
perhaps it is only me.
Be light, for my voice is heavy.
The corpses have grown calm.

Have I yet enough space
for an intelligent death?
—A man who knew nothing about it
discovered the central fire.

Mex[ico City], April [19]45.

It takes . . .

It takes men without faces,
it takes faces without men,
clamor without depth
and torture without value.

And let steaming rains fall
on the cerebral jungle!
So many funerary masks
are preserved in the earth
that nothing yet is lost.

Mex[ico City], April [19]45

After that splendid Notre Dame . . .

For L.
"Don't be sad . . ."

After that splendid Notre Dame inverted
in a Seine pure of the clochards' remorse,
after that trembling rose window abloom in the dark water
where the stars spin out their inconceivable threads
across profiles of sea horses and foliage as real as mirages,

what remains, oh my madly reasonable spirit,

what still remains inaccessible to the wide-awake sleeper
who follows down these dark quays, from one Commune to
    the next,
the hope-filled cortege of his executed brothers?

Paris, 1938

It's salt water that quenches . . .

It's salt water that quenches the thirst for blood, oh bitter
war!

Handsome faces and dirty mugs are made for the same
wounds,
brave hearts and cowardly souls are made for the same
tortures,
and all their eyes will be put out, and all their bellies ripped
open, and all their sexes torn apart
by the fine teeth of machines that glitter like galaxies.

All the cities I have known, all the unknown cities
drift, cracked ice floes, toward the most barren dawns.
Will they survive, will we? Oh world entire, desirable world,
our vessel so dismasted, world of turbines and panthers,
world of decapitated ideas, will we survive, will they?

Trinitrotoluene explodes into nebulas in the brain,
the song of blood on metals turns into a dazzling word,
there are smiles beneath the helmets, smiles as hard as
knives
—all the moorings will be cut, the wounds of the dead will
be washed,
that is as sure as the darkness.

We only need patience! The song of the veins, that is
patience.
Let bitter fruit ripen, nourished on sand and venom.
The survivors' burning throats! We will gladly drink
the darkest saps! Those of exhausting punishments, of
obsessions, of rancors . . .
The blind nights are powerful, and we are their patience.

Mexico City, [19]43.

III. Mains/Hands

Mains

Terre cuite d'un artiste italien du XVIe siècle, parfois
attribuée à Michel-Ange — Musée de Londres.

Quel contact étonnant, vieil homme, établissent tes mains
    avec les nôtres!
Que les siècles de mort sont vains devant tes mains . . .

L'artiste sans nom comme toi les a surprises dans un
    mouvement de prise
dont on ne sait s'il vibre encore ou s'il vient de s'éteindre,
Les veines battent, ce sont des vieilles veines durcies par le
    chant du sang,
ah, que prennent-elles, tes mains de vigueur finissante,
s'agrippent-elles à la terre, s'agrippent-elles à la chair,
la dernière ou l'avant-dernière fois,
ramassent-elles le cristal qui contient la pureté,
caressent-elles l'ombre vivante qui contient la fécondité,
sont-elles de patience,
sont-elles d'acharnement, d'ardeur, de résistance,
sont-elles secrètement de défaillance?
Le certain, c'est leur fierté.

Les veines de tes mains, vieil homme, expriment la prière,
la prière de ton sang, vieil homme, l'avant-dernière prière,
non la prière verbale, non la prière cléricale,
mais celle de l'ardeur pensante,
puissante—impuissante.
Leur présence confronte le monde avec lui-même,
elle l'interroge comme on interroge ce qu'on aime
définitivement
sans que la réponse soit possible.

Hands

*Terra-cotta by a sixteenth-century Italian artist, sometimes
attributed to Michelangelo – London Museum.*

What astonishing contact, old man, your hands establish
    with our own!
How vain the centuries of death next to your hands . . .

The artist, nameless like you, surprised them in the act of
    grasping
—who knows whether the gesture still quivers or has just
    now died away,
The veins throb, they are old veins toughened by the song of
    the blood,
ah, but what are they grasping, your hands with their failing
    strength,
are they clinging to the earth, are they clinging to flesh,
for the last or the next-to-last time,
are they picking up the crystal that contains purity,
are they caressing the living shadow that contains fecundity,
are they hands of patience,
are they hands of determination, fervor, resistance,
are they secretly hands of weakness?
The only thing certain is their pride.

The veins of your hands, old man, express prayer,
the prayer of your blood, old man, the next-to-last prayer,
not verbal prayer, not clerical prayer,
but the prayer of reasoning fervor,
powerful—powerless.
Their presence confronts the world with itself,
their presence questions it as one questions what one loves
definitively
with no possible response.

Suis-je seul, moi sourd, moi tellement séparé de toi,
moi tellement détaché de moi,
suis-je seul à savoir comme tu es seul,
moi seul à cet instant et si tendu vers toi
dans le temps?

Ou sommes-nous seuls ensemble
parmi tous ceux dans la durée qui sont seuls avec nous,
formant le chœur unique qui murmure dans nos veines
    communes,
nos veines chantantes?

J'ai pensé à te dire, vieil homme, une chose émouvante,
émue,
fraternelle,
à trouver pour toi, au nom de tous les autres, une parole nue
d'aurore boréale
de lueur sur les glaciers,
une parole simple, intime et loyale.

Toi, tu ne savais pas
que les veines des tempes des électrocutés
bouillonnent comme des nœuds de sang révolté
sous la peau ruisselante d'une sueur plus atroce que la sueur
    du Christ sur la croix.
Quelqu'un m'a dit qu'il pensa en voyant ça
à une mouche proie d'une étrange araignée
et la mouche était une âme pardonnée.

Ah, que pourrais-je, ah que pourrais-je pour soulager tes
    veines,
moi qui sais les supplices, toi qui sais les supplices,
il faut pourtant que nous puissions l'un pour l'autre,
d'un bout du temps à l'autre,
jeter dans les balances inexorables de l'univers
au moins la fragilité d'une pensée, d'un signe, d'un vers

Am I alone, deaf as I am and so far removed from you,
so detached as I am from myself,
am I alone in knowing how alone you are,
I so alone at this moment and reaching out to you
through time?

Or are we alone together
with all those who in the course of time are alone with us,
forming the unique chorus that murmurs in our shared
     veins,
our singing veins?

I thought of telling you, old man, something moving,
moved,
fraternal,
of finding for you, in the name of all the others, a naked
     word
of the northern lights,
of the glow on the glaciers,
a simple, intimate, loyal word.

But you did not know
that the veins in the temples of the electrocuted
boil like knots of rebellious blood
under the skin running with sweat more appalling than the
     sweat of Christ on the cross.
Someone told me the sight reminded him
of a fly stalked by a strange spider
and the fly was a forgiven soul.

What could I do, ah, what could I do to soothe your veins,
I who know torments, you who know torments,
and yet we must be capable each of us for the other,
from one end of time to the other,
of throwing onto the inexorable scales of the universe
at least the fragility of a thought, a sign, a line of verse

qui n'a peut-être ni substance ni radiance mais qui est,
aussi réel que les veines implorantes de ta main,
que les veines des miennes si peu différentes . . .

Que la dernière lueur de la dernière aurore,
que la dernière étoile intermittente,
que la dernière détresse de la dernière attente,
que la dernière sourire du masque rasséréné,
soient sur les veines de ta main, vieil homme rencontré.

Une goutte de sang tombe d'un ciel à l'autre,
éblouissante.

Nos mains sont d'inconscience, de dureté, d'ascension, de
    conscience,
de plain-chant, de souffrance ravie,
clouées aux arcs-en-ciel.
Ensemble, ensemble, unies,
voici qu'elles ont saisi
l'inespéré.

Et nous ne savions pas
que nous tenions ensemble
cet éblouissement.

Une goute de sang—
un seul trait de lumière tombe d'une main à l'autre,
éblouissant.

Mexico, novembre 1947.

that has perhaps neither substance nor radiance yet exists,
as real as the imploring veins of your hand,
as real as the veins of mine so little different . . .

Let the final glow of the final dawn,
let the final intermittent star,
let the final distress in the final waiting,
let the final smile on the serene mask
fall on the veins of your hand, old man whom I have just
    found.

A drop of blood falls from one sky to another,
dazzling.

Our hands are made of unconsciousness, of hardness, of
    ascension, of consciousness,
of plainchant, of ravished suffering,
our hands nailed to rainbows.
Together, joined together,
here they have laid hold of
the unhoped-for.

And we did not know
that together we held
this dazzling thing.

A drop of blood—
a single shaft of light falls from one hand to the other,
dazzling.

Mexico City, November 1947.

Notes to the Poems

Many of the notes are based on Jean Rière's notes in his edition of the poems: Victor Serge, *Pour un brasier dans un désert* (Bassac [Charente], France: Plein Chant, 1998), although with selection, condensation, and sometimes extension; these notes are marked (JR). Unattributed notes are by the translator. Some notes reference and quote from Serge's notebooks: *Carnets (1936–1947)*, édition établie par Claudio Albertani et Claude Rioux (Marseille: Agone, 2012). The transliteration of personal names usually conforms to that in Serge's *Memoirs of a Revolutionary*, Peter Sedgwick with George Paizis, trans. (New York: New York Review Books, 2012), which is a major source for notes. For more on Serge's son, Vladimir Kibalchich Russakov, called Vlady (1920–2005), see the rich documentation on Jean-Guy Rens's site at http://www.vlady.org.

I. Resistance

Résistance was first published as an issue of *Les Humbles*, nos. 11–12 (Paris, 1938), in a limited edition; this collection was reprinted as *Pour un brasier dans un désert* (Paris: François Maspéro, 1972) and as *Résistance: Poèmes* (Geneva: Éditions Héros-Limite, 2016). The original manuscript was confiscated by the secret police as Serge left the Soviet Union after being freed from deportation (1933–1936) in Orenburg, on the Ural River near the Russia–Kazakhstan border. (Other manuscripts that were confiscated and not found again in the state archives include the novels *Les Hommes perdus* [The Fallen], about the anarchist milieu before the First World War, and *La Tourmente* [The Storm], about the Russian Civil War.) After his arrival in the West, Serge recreated some of the poems from memory; other poems had been mailed to friends and published in journals abroad.

All the dedicatees were in the anti-Stalin Opposition and died either in the camps or during the Moscow Trials, which had begun soon after Serge's release. Boris Mikhailovich Eltsin (1875–1936?), a Bolshevik since 1903, was an old comrade of Lenin's; Chanaan Markovich Pevzner was a Muscovite worker in the Opposition in 1927–1928; Vassily Mikhailovich Chernykh was a former Red Army commissar; Yakov Belenky (1885–1938) was a history professor; Ivan Byk was a Ukrainian tanner and Trotskyist; Boris Ilyich Lakovitski was an Oppositionist tailor from Minsk; Alexei Semionovich Santalov, a turner from Leningrad, was arrested for calling Stalin "this gravedigger of the Revolution" in a workers' club (*Memoirs*, 361); Lydia Svalova was a courageous young worker from Perm; and Fayna Upstein, from Odessa, was in the 1927 Opposition. Nesterov, the former chief of staff of the president of the Council of People's Commissars, was a cellmate of Serge's in 1933, shortly before Serge was deported to Orenburg (*Memoirs*, 343). No information is available on Yegorich. Serge's novel *Midnight in the Century* captures the "spiritual atmosphere" of the deportation (Richard Greeman, trans. [New York: New York Review Books, 2015]). The epigraph is from Charles Péguy's *Eve*. (JR) Rière's sources, which sometimes differ on details, include Serge's "Les déportés d'Orenbourg [1936]," *Cahiers Léon Trotsky*, nos. 7–8 (Paris, 1981): 221–228; *Destin d'une Révolution* (1937), in *Russia Twenty Years After*, Max Schachtman, trans. (Atlantic Highlands, NJ: Humanities Press, 1996), 107–110; and *Memoirs*, 356–361.

Frontier, p. 31
Sent by Serge to his friend Henry Poulaille on 25 September 1934. First published in *Le Rouge et le Noir*, no. 222 (Brussels, 12 December 1934). Published by Poulaille in the literary weekly *Les Feuillets bleus*, no. 295 (Paris, 15 May 1935): 627, a special issue dedicated to Serge. (JR)

Henry Poulaille (1896–1980) was a French writer who furthered the cause of what he called proletarian literature, in opposition to socialist realism, through the many journals he edited and published. A key organizer of the international campaign for Serge's release from captivity in the Soviet Union, Poulaille was later a member of the Committee for Inquiry into the Moscow Trials and the Defense of Free Speech in the Revolution. Serge praised Poulaille as "a true son of the workers' suburbs who did not mince his words" (*Memoirs*, 370).
yet not so high as the pursuit plane: At the time of Serge's deportation, Orenburg was the site of an air base.
Frisco where the IWWs live: The San Francisco General Strike took place in July 1934, before the probable date of composition of "Frontier." The Industrial Workers of the World (IWW), a revolutionary union in the United States, flourished between 1905 and the end of the First World War.

People of the Ural, p. 34
First published in *Almanach populaire*, no. 1 (Paris, 1937): 279–280, an organ of the French Socialist Party. (JR)

"for in this world . . .": Serge quotes (in English in the original) from memory this line of Oscar Wilde's "The Ballad of Reading Gaol": "Yet each man kills the thing he loves." (JR)

Puvis's gray landscape: Pierre Puvis de Chavannes, painter of *The Poor Fisherman*, to which Serge alludes here. (JR)

what is happening in Asturias: In October 1934, the miners of Asturias, Spain, took up arms against the right-wing government in what "one may regard . . . as the first battle of the Civil War," which began in earnest two years later. The state repression that followed the fighting included thousands of summary executions, many incidents of torture, and some 40,000 sent to prison (Gerald Brenan, *The Spanish Labyrinth* [London: Cambridge University Press, 1960], 284–289).

Old Woman, p. 37
Sent by Serge to Poulaille on 13 July 1934, who published it in his review *À Contre courant*, no. 1 (Paris, July 1935): 40; reprinted in *Almanach populaire*, no. 11 (Paris, 1938): 253. (JR)

Somewhere else . . ., p. 38
Published in *Almanach populaire*, no. 11 (Paris, 1938): 130. (JR)

Just Four Girls, p. 40
Sent by Serge to Poulaille on 11 September 1934; published in *Révolution prolétarienne*, no. 188 (Paris, 10 December 1934): 11–12; published by Poulaille in *Les Feuillets bleus*, no. 295 (Paris, 15 May 1935): 628. (JR)

where all is but "order . . .": Serge quotes from memory from Charles Baudelaire's "L'invitation au voyage": "Là, tout n'est qu'ordre et beauté, / Luxe, calme et volupté."

The Asphyxiated Man, p. 43
Sent by Serge to Poulaille on 13 July 1934. (JR)

with Chapayev, with Furmanov: Vassily Ivanovich Chapayev (1887–1919) was a peasant who became a leader of the Red Army and a hero of the Civil War. Dimitri Andreivich Furmanov (1891–1926) was political commissar of the Chapayev Division (1919–1921) and a novelist whose works include *Chapayev* (1923). (JR) A popular film based on the novel was released in 1934 (Mitchell Abidor, private communication).

Tiflis, p. 46
Rustaveli's verses: Shota Rustaveli (1172–1216) was a Georgian poet, author of the national epic, *The Knight in the Panther's Skin*. (JR)

On 11 September 1934, Serge sent parts I and II to Poulaille, who published them in *Les Feuillets bleus,* no. 295 (Paris, 15 May 1935); part I also appeared in *Europe,* no. 145 (Paris, 15 January 1935): 61–62. (JR)

I. *Alexis Mikhaylovich*

In this translation, the title of this part is restored from the table of contents of the original edition of *Résistance* (1938).

Czar Alexis Mikhaylovich (1629–1676), the second prince of the Romanovs, began his reign in 1645. In 1648, he married Mariya Miloslavskaya, by whom he had eight daughters and five sons, including Alexis Alekseyevich (1654–1670), Fydor Alekseyevich (1657–1682, czar under the name of Fydor III), and Ivan Alekseyevich (1666–1696, feebleminded). In 1671, he married Natalia Narychkina (1651–1694), by whom he had Pyotr (Peter) Alekseyevich (1672–1725). Ivan and Peter were named czars in 1682, under the tutelage of their sister Sophia Alekseyevna (1657–1704), who was regent until 1689, when Peter overthrew her and became Peter the Great. His son Alexis Petrovich (1690–1718) opposed his reforms, so Peter had him arrested; he was left to die in prison. (JR)

a pale Ophelia: Euphemia Vsevolozhkaya, dolled up and presented to the czar, was overcome by emotion and misgiving, and fainted. She and her family were deported. (JR)

pure-hearted Natalya: Natalya Kirillovna Naryshkina was the ward of Prime Minister Artamon Matveyev, who was concerned with ensuring his own power. She was presented to the czar on 11 February 1670. Intrigues by the Miloslavsky clan delayed the marriage for nine months. (JR)

the incorruptible patriarch: Nikon (1605–1681), for a time a favorite of Czar Alexis Mikhaylovich, was dismissed and exiled in 1666. He was a partisan of liturgical reforms that resulted in a schism whose guiding spirit was "the steadfast heresiarch," Avvakum (1620–1682). Avvakum was exiled in 1653 and 1664, then burned alive. (JR)

II. *Stenka Razin*

Stenka Razin: Stepan Timofeyevich Razin (c. 1630–1671), a Don Cossack, was the illustrious chief of the peasant revolt of 1670–1671. In October 1670, he was defeated near Simbirsk by the armies of Czar Alexis Mikhaylovich, then betrayed and handed over in April 1671. With his brother Frol, he was executed in Moscow that June. (JR)

Tom Mooney: A radical San Francisco labor leader wrongfully charged with participation in the bombing of the 1916 Preparedness Day parade, which advocated American involvement in the First World War. In the highly politicized trial, he and Warren Billings were convicted and

sentenced to death. In response to an international campaign, the sentences were commuted to life imprisonment in 1918. The campaign for their release continued; they were pardoned and set free only in 1939.
Saragossa general strike: In March 1934, the anarchist Confederación Nacional del Trabajo (CNT) in Saragossa, Spain, called a general strike "as a protest against the bad treatment of the prisoners taken in the previous December" during an insurrection against the newly installed right-wing government (Brenan, *Spanish Labyrinth*, 271).
Congress of the United Federation of Teachers: At this August 1934 conference in Montpellier, France, two schoolteachers introduced a successful resolution in favor of Victor Serge. (JR)
Koloman Wallisch: A member of the Austrian Social Democratic Party, Wallisch was hanged, with eight others, for his participation in the 12 February 1934 uprising in Vienna against the authoritarian Dollfuss government. As he died, he shouted: "Long live social democracy! Freedom!" (JR)

III. *Confessions*
Inspired by the "confessions" at the three Moscow Trials (1936, 1937, 1938) organized by Stalin. (JR)

Boat on the Ural, p. 57
Dedicated to "Henry Poulaille fraternellement V. S." and dated Orenburg, 20 May 1935; published in Poulaille's review *À Contre courant*, no. 11 (Paris, May 1936): 97–99. (JR)

Tête-à-Tête, p. 60
You whom they welcomed: A reference to Serge's wife, Liuba Russakova (1898–1984), who was diagnosed with schizophrenia and eventually institutionalized, first in the Soviet Union and later in Marseille, where she died. With her family, Liuba had emigrated from Russia to Marseille (1908–1919) after the 1905 pogroms. Returning to Russia on the same ship as Serge in February 1919, she soon became his companion. Her psychiatric problems first appeared in 1930. (JR)

From the late 1920s on, the persecution of the anti-Stalin Opposition to which Serge belonged grew ever more severe:

> In this atmosphere my wife lost her reason. I found her one evening lying in bed with a medical dictionary in her hand, calm but ravaged. "I have just read the article on madness. I know that I am going mad. Wouldn't I be better off dead?" . . . I took her to psychiatrists, who were generally excellent men, and she settled down in the clinics . . . She would come home again a little better for a while, and then the old story began

again: ration cards refused, denunciations, arrests, death sentences demanded over all the loudspeakers placed at the street corners. (*Memoirs*, 320–321)

During a period of remission in 1934, Liuba briefly joined Serge and their teenage son, Vlady, in exile in Orenburg before relapsing and returning to the mental hospital (492).

In "Le nuage intérieur," 17 juin 1941, *Carnets*, 101, Serge writes, in an entry addressed to Laurette Séjourné, who had not yet joined him in Mexico:

> I will not go mad. I am destined to remain implacably lucid, and I would be even intolerably so if I did not have a tragic sense of life that is almost childish. I've so often skirted the borders of madness that I've become convinced of the impossibility of my crossing them—and I am the author of this strength, having seen up close the indescribable defeat of the mind and the unimaginable suffering that comes with it (Liuba).

Skardanelli: Gaston Ferdière, a psychiatrist who wanted to shed light on Liuba's condition, had sent Serge a copy of *Poèmes de la folie d'Hölderlin* (Poems of Hölderlin's Madness), translated by Pierre-Jean Jouve and Pierre Klossowski. (JR) Friedrich Hölderlin signed some of his last poems with the name Skardanelli or Scardanelli and gave them seemingly random dates, e.g., 9 March 1940.

On the splendor of man: My rendering of the French translation of the first line of Hölderlin's "Griechenland": "Wie Menschen sind, so ist das Leben prächtig." The poem is signed Scardanelli and dated 24 May 1748.

Dialectic, p. 62

I.

desperate Communards: Defenders of the Paris Commune (18 March–28 May 1871), a radically democratic, socialist uprising against the French government at the close of the Franco-Prussian War. Toward the end of the fighting, many Communards were shot against a wall of the Père Lachaise cemetery.

Versaillais: Soldiers in the regular French army that put down the Commune.

the Cheka: The All-Russian Extraordinary Commission was the Soviet security apparatus formed at the beginning of the revolution.

II.

Monsieur le Marquis de Galliffet: General Gaston de Galliffet, notorious as the suppressor of the Paris Commune.

III.

They perish exactly as: Incidents of the September Massacres in Paris, which were triggered by the fall of the fortress of Verdun to the invading Prussians on 2 September 1792 (Peter McPhee, *The French Revolution 1789–1799* [Oxford: Oxford University Press, 2002], 98).

La Force: A prison in Paris.

Citizen Billaud: Jacques Nicolas Billaud-Varenne (1756–1819), a Jacobin orator known for his fiery diatribes. (JR)

Constellation of Dead Brothers, p. 66

Written at the time (1933–1934) that Serge was also writing his novel *Les Hommes perdus* (The Fallen), the poem evokes friends who died tragically. André Brode was a Latvian sailor and revolutionary whom Serge met in the French concentration camp in Précigné, Sarthe, where Serge was held (1918–1919) at the end of the First World War. Brode died fighting the Whites in defense of Riga in 1919. "Dario" is Salvador Seguí, a Catalan CNT leader, who was killed in 1923 in Barcelona by the ultraright or the police. (On Seguí and the struggle in Barcelona, see *Memoirs*, 60–68, and Serge's novel *Birth of Our Power* [Richard Greeman, trans. (New York: New York Review Books, 2011)], where Seguí is fictionalized as "Dario.") "Boris" is probably Dimitri Barakov, a sailor and syndicalist whom Serge met in Précigné. In 1919 Serge and Barakov sailed to the Soviet Union in a postwar hostage exchange; Barakov died of tuberculosis soon after arrival. (See notes to "Max" below.) "David" is another acquaintance from Précigné, Aaron Zieplinck, a young Russian who was killed during an escape attempt in 1918. "Karl" is Vladimir Ossipovich Lichtenstadt-Mazin, a colleague and close friend of Serge's in the press section in the early days of the Communist International, who died on the front during the Civil War. (According to a note in *Memoirs*, 481, Serge named his son Vlady after Mazin.) "The Four" are the writer and Communist activist Raymond Lefebvre, the anarcho-syndicalist Jules Marius Lepetit (Louis Alexandre Bertho), the revolutionary syndicalist activist Marcel Vergeat, and their Russian interpreter Sasha Tubin (Sasha Mitkovitser). Having come to Moscow for the Second Congress of the Third International (1920), on their return voyage they died in mysterious circumstances off Murmansk in the Arctic Ocean. Vassily Nikiforovich Chadayev was a Communist activist in Leningrad (1917–1928). (See notes to "26 August 28" below.) Nguyen Ai Quoc was the pseudonym of Nguyen Tat Thanh, later known as Ho Chi Minh, founder of the Vietminh and the first president of Vietnam; at the time of Serge's writing, the Communist press had mistakenly reported his death in prison. René Valet, a locksmith and deserter, a member of the Bonnot Gang (an anarchist group led by Jules Bonnot), was killed by the police after an epic siege (1912).

Raymond Callemin, Serge's boyhood friend and also a member of the Bonnot Gang, was guillotined (1913). (JR)

In this translation, the word "camerado" is borrowed from Whitman, whose "As I lay with my head in your lap, Camerado" resonates with "Constellation of Dead Brothers": "Dear camerado! I confess I have urged you onward with me, and still urge you, without the least idea what is our destination, / Or whether we shall be victorious, or utterly quell'd and defeated" (Walt Whitman, *Drum-Taps: The Complete 1865 Edition*, Lawrence Kramer, ed. [New York: New York Review Books, 2015], 123).

Max, p. 68
Sent by Serge on 5 July 1931 to Poulaille, who published it as "Pour un mort" (For a Dead Man) in his review *Nouvel Âge*, no. 9 (Paris, September 1931): 828–829. "Max" is probably Dimitri Barakov, the "Boris" of "Constellation of Dead Brothers," who died of tuberculosis in 1919, soon after he and Serge arrived in the Soviet Union. (JR)

City, p. 72
Published, with "26 August 28," in *Le Journal des Poètes*, no. 9 (Brussels, 5 February 1933): 3, to which they were sent on 1 December 1932; reprinted by Poulaille in *Les Feuillets bleus*, no. 295 (Paris, 15 May 1935): 625–626. (JR)

Serge also evokes Petrograd, now St. Petersburg, in *Revolution in Danger: Writings from Russia 1919–1921*, Ian Birchall, trans. (Chicago: Haymarket Books, 1997) and in *Conquered City*, Richard Greeman, trans. (New York: Doubleday, 1975).

26 August 28, p. 74
See the publication facts for "City."

The poem recalls the death of a close friend and comrade, Vassily Nikiforovich Chadayev, also evoked in "Constellation of Dead Brothers." (JR) In 1928, Chadayev was arrested at the same time as Serge for being a Left Oppositionist. After his release from prison and en route to Kuban on an official mission, Chadayev visited Serge at Detskoye Selo: "We spent several hours rowing on the lake . . . Vassily Nikiforovich sang me the praises of prison, that benevolent retreat where a man takes stock of himself" (*Memoirs*, 281). Serge describes Chadayev's murder under suspicious circumstances while investigating corruption in Kuban:

> All I ever saw of him again were some dreadful photographs:
> the dumdum bullets, fired from sawn-off rifles, had harrowed
> his face and chest monstrously . . . A stone with an inscription,

erected on the spot where he died, was broken into fragments. (282)

We must be strong: In "Marseille," 24 mars 1941, *Carnets*, 57, Serge quotes this stanza in the context of temporarily leaving Laurette Séjourné behind as he sets sail from Marseille on his journey into exile in Mexico. *Detskoye Selo:* Site of an imperial residence outside Petrograd, frequented by poets and writers, including Serge's friends Andrei Bely, author of *Petersburg* (1922), and Fyodor Sologub, author of *The Petty Demon* (1907) (*Memoirs*, 314).

Death of Panait, p. 76

Panait Istrati (1884–1935), a Francophone Romanian novelist born in Brăila, was a great friend and defender of Serge. Serge met Istrati in November 1927 in the company of Nikos Kazantzakis (1883–1957). Both writers had been invited to celebrate the tenth anniversary of the October Revolution, with Istrati staying sixteen months in the Soviet Union. On his return to Europe, Istrati published his *Vers l'autre flamme* (Toward the Other Flame) trilogy with Rieder (1929), which contains devastating critiques of emerging Stalinism and its effects on society. Although all three volumes were signed by Istrati, he is the author of only volume 1, *Après seize mois dans l'U.R.S.S.* (After Sixteen Months in the USSR). Volume 2, *Soviets 1929*, is by Serge, and volume 3, *La Russie nue*, is by Boris Souvarine. (JR)

"Death of Panait" was written in Orenburg in 1935 but confiscated as Serge was leaving the Soviet Union in April 1936. In Brussels, Serge recomposed the poem from memory on 24 December 1936. In 1937, he gave the poem to Eleni Samios (the wife of Nikos Kazantzakis) to preface her book *La Véritable tragédie de Panaït Istrati* (The True Tragedy of Panait Istrati), which saw publication only in Spanish as *La Verdadera Tragedia de Panait Istrati*, Luis Alberto Sánchez, trans. (Santiago de Chile: Ediciones Ercilla, 1938). (JR) The French original of the book (minus the prefatory poem) was finally published in Eleni Samios-Kazantzaki, *La Véritable tragédie de Panaït Istrati*, édition établie par Maria Teresa Ricci et Anselm Jappe (Fécamp, France: Nouvelles Éditions Lignes, 2013), with Serge's letters of 1929–1932 to Istrati. *the Salt Lake Inn:* The Hotel Bobesco in Istrati's *Méditerranée (Coucher du soleil)*. (JR) *Nerrantsoula:* The heroine of Istrati's novel of the same name. (JR) *at Rieder's:* Éditions Rieder published works by Istrati and Serge, including Serge's first three novels: *Men in Prison* (1930) (preface by Istrati), *Birth of Our Power* (1930), and *Conquered City* (1932). A friend of Serge's, the poet Marcel Martinet, was for a time the literary director at Rieder (George Paizis, *Marcel Martinet: Poet of the Revolution* [London:

Francis Boutle, 2008], 242). For more on Martinet, see the notes to "Mexico: Idyll."

your Baragan: Romanian steppe evoked in Istrati's *Les Chardons du Baragan*, translated by Jacques Le Clerc as *The Thistles of the Baragan* (New York: The Vanguard Press, 1930). (JR)

Why Inscribe a Name?, p. 81

Published by Poulaille in *Les Feuillets bleus*, no. 295 (Paris, 15 May 1935): 628. (JR)

The title might be an allusion to the death of Serge's friend Vassily Nikiforovich Chadayev, memorialized in "Constellation of Dead Brothers" and "26 August 28," but the question foreshadows Serge's own eventual burial in a common grave in Mexico two decades on.

Koktebel: A cultural center in the Crimea, presided over by the Symbolist poet Maximilian Voloshin, whom Serge and his family had visited in 1932. (JR)

Cassiopeia, p. 82

Tatiana: According to Vlady, a Cossack nurse with whom Serge was romantically involved in Orenburg. (JR)

Song, p. 84

The epigraph is from Guillaume Apollinaire's "La chanson du mal-aimé," in his *Alcools*. Like Apollinaire's equally mysterious poem, Serge's original is in five-line stanzas of rhymed octosyllabics. The first couplet of "Song" appears as the beginning of a poem in progress composed by Félicien Mûrier, a character in Victor Serge, *The Long Dusk*, Ralph Manheim, trans. (New York: The Dial Press, 1946), 153. The last stanza appears as written by an unnamed poet in Victor Serge, *The Case of Comrade Tulayev*, Willard R. Trask, trans. (Garden City, NY: Doubleday, 1950), 294. For Apollinaire's poem, see "The Song of the Poorly Loved," in Guillaume Apollinaire, *Alcools*, Anne Hyde Greet, trans. (Berkeley: University of California Press, 1965), 16–37.

Trust, p. 86

Sent to Poulaille on 25 September 1934 and published in *Les Feuillets bleus*, no. 295 (15 May 1935): 628; published in René Lefeuvre's *Spartacus*, no. 2 (Paris, Friday, 14 December 1934): 5. (JR)

the nonextended: Possibly a reference to Descartes's distinction between the "extended" body and the "nonextended" mind.

Sensation, p. 88

For L . . .: Laurette Séjourné, (1911–2003), Serge's companion from 1937 till his death in 1947. The dedication is in English in the original.

II. Messages

At his death, Serge left this unpublished collection as a typed manuscript with the "provisional title" of *Messages* (1946). Jean Rière received a copy of the manuscript from Léo Moulin (1906–1996), a sociologist and the husband of the poet Jeanine Moulin. Léo Moulin had received the manuscript from Jef Rens (1905–1985), an official in the International Labor Organization in Brussels and Geneva; Rens had received the manuscript from Serge. (JR) *Messages* was first published in Rière's edition of Serge's poems. In Rière's estimation, the collection translated here is only part of a lost manuscript that contained ten additional poems.

"Messages" is also the title of a chapter of Serge's *Midnight in the Century*. In his introduction, Greeman notes that messages "are an important theme in the novel" (xx) as they circulate among Oppositionists in the Gulag, nourishing "the novel's heroes with information, ideas, and hope, reminding them that they are not alone" (xxii).

Sunday, p. 91

oh life is so beautiful: "Ah, que la vie est belle" (1911) is a chansonnette by the singer and songwriter Doralys (d. 1934) (Renée Morel, private communication).

Bérangère, p. 93

Published, thanks to Jeanine Moulin, in *Le Journal des Poètes*, 28e année, no. 1 (Brussels, 1958): 10. (JR)

The poem seems to reflect the style of Jehan Rictus (1867–1933); my free translation of "Bérangère" tries to convey a similar style and feeling. Rictus was a post-Symbolist poet who, in the years before the First World War, wrote poems of the down-and-out (notably, *Les Soliloques du Pauvre* [1903] [The Poor Man's Soliloquies]), reciting them in Parisian cabarets and other public venues. For a time, he led a vagabond existence in the city and was close to the prewar anarchists. (See Herbert W. Kitson, *Les Soliloques du Pauvre de Jehan Rictus: Translation with Introduction and Notes* [Washington, DC: University Press of America, 1982].) Serge admired his work: "Jehan Rictus lamented the suffering of the penniless intellectual dragging out his nights on the benches of foreign boulevards" (*Memoirs*, 21). The final stanza echoes a chantey in Serge, *Conquered City*, 102: "Every ship will go to the bottom / Sixty fathoms deep! / Who gives a damn! Who gives a damn!"

Suicide of Dr. C., p. 94

"C." is probably Dr. Gaëtan Gatian de Clérambault, a psychiatrist who, depressed and fearful of going blind after a cataract operation, shot himself on 17 November 1934. (JR)

How Clérambault figures in Serge's life is unclear. Clérambault does play a part in the controversy surrounding André Breton's attack on the psychiatric profession in *Nadja* (1928). In 1930, Breton's *Second Manifesto of Surrealism* begins with an excerpt of the proceedings of a professional meeting where Clérambault and others respond to Breton with a critique of Surrealism. Clérambault was also an early mentor to Jacques Lacan, whose involvement with Surrealism included publishing in *Minotaure* in the 1930s. At least something of this history would have been known to Serge. Interestingly, Clérambault, like Serge, compares Surrealism to Gongorism.

Given its date of composition, the poem more properly belongs in *Resistance*. In "Mort d'Otto et Alice Rühle," 24 juin 1943, *Carnets*, 345, Serge remembers Alice Rühle reading "a poem of mine, 'Suicide of Dr. C.,' written in Orenburg in 1934, that I had forgotten and then suddenly recreated in one hour in Mexico City while walking in the rain in 1941."

Curiously, Serge described a similar suicide scene in *Memoirs* in 1942–1943, where he imagines the suicide of his friend and comrade Adolf Abramovich Joffe (1883–1927), who kills himself in despair at the turn the Russian Revolution had taken under Stalin:

> Brief meditation: wife, child, city; the huge eternal universe; and myself about to go . . . Now to do quickly and well what has been irrevocably decided: press the automatic comfortably against the temple, there will be a shock and no pain at all. Shock, then nothing. (267)

a devastated shade: A reference to Serge's wife, Liuba Russakova. (JR)

Marseille, p. 96

Published by Roger Caillois in *Lettres françaises/Cahiers trimestriels de littérature française, édités par les soins de la revue SUR avec la collaboration des écrivains français résidant en France et à l'étranger*, no. 4 (Buenos Aires, 1 April 1942): 15–16. The influential literary journal *Sur* was published by Victoria Ocampo. (JR)

As France fell to the invading German army in 1940, Serge fled from Paris to Marseille, where he found refuge with Varian Fry's Emergency Rescue Committee. (JR)

Planet without visas: Perhaps an echo of the title of a chapter in Trotsky's *My Life* (1930).

Moscou Vienne Berlin: Serge updates a fifteenth-century song that is known to every French child, "Le Carillon de Vendôme" (The Chimes of Vendôme). Its refrain—"Orléans, Beaugency, / Notre-Dame de Cléry, / Vendôme, Vendôme!"—commemorates places in the Loire region that at a certain point in the Hundred Years' War remained to the future Charles VII, who was under dire threat from the invading

English and the Burgundians. Moscow, Vienna, Berlin, and Barcelona were important in Serge's life as sites of revolt, revolution, and triumphant counterrevolution (Stalin, Dollfuss, Hitler, Franco). At the end of the Franco-Prussian War, the Parc Montsouris saw extensive fighting during the Paris Commune (1871), which was savagely suppressed by French government forces; Paris fell to the Germans in 1940. Serge would have been aware of the relevance of the modern history of towns mentioned in "Le Carillon de Vendôme": Orléans was occupied by the Prussians in the Franco-Prussian War and then by the Germans in the Second World War. Cléry-Saint-André, home to the Basilica of Notre-Dame de Cléry, suffered at the hands of the Prussians in the Franco-Prussian War. The mention of Vendôme foreshadows the destruction centuries later of the Vendôme column by revolutionaries of the Paris Commune, as well as the German bombing of the town of Vendôme in 1940. See, with a grain of salt, the Wikipédia articles "Le Carillon de Vendôme," "Parc Montsouris," "Orléans," "Beaugency," "Cléry-Saint-André," "Basilique Notre-Dame de Cléry-Saint-André," and "Vendôme" at http://fr.wikipedia.org.

The rats are leaving . . . , p. 98

Published in *Lettres françaises*, no. 4 (Buenos Aires, 1 April 1942): 17–18; reprinted in *Le Journal des Poètes*, no. 1 (Brussels, 1958): 10. (JR)

Out at Sea, p. 100

For L.: Laurette Séjourné, Serge's companion, remained in France when Serge and Vlady escaped on a ship out of Marseille. She joined them in Mexico a year later, bringing with her Serge's five-year-old daughter Jeannine (Richard Greeman, private communication).

The Cuban artist: Wifredo Lam (1902–1982) had a Chinese father and a Cuban mother. Like Serge, Lam was a refugee in Marseille. On 25 March 1941, Lam left France on the *Capitaine Paul-Lemerle* along with, among others, Serge and Vlady, André Breton, and Claude Lévi-Strauss. (JR) Lam had "fought in the Spanish Civil War . . . Through Picasso he was introduced" to Breton and the Surrealist group in Paris (Lowery Stokes Sims, *Wifredo Lam and the International Avant-Garde, 1923–1982* [Austin: University of Texas Press, 2002], 3).

In the brisk air of departure: In "Marseille," 24 mars 1941, *Carnets*, 56–57, Serge addresses Séjourné as he writes of his and Vlady's departure from Marseille; at the end of the entry he slightly misquotes from "26 August 28," written many years before:

> Left around 1:30, for a long while we watch Marseille growing ever more distant, Notre-Dame-de-la-Garde, the transporter bridge, our memories. Soft golden evening, thinking of your

solitude, I suppress a rout. "We must be strong / we must be hard / I will go on / but really, that's hard . . ."

the Brûleur de Loups: A café-brasserie on the Quai des Belges at the Old Port of Marseille. Among its habitués were Breton, Jacqueline Lamba, Benjamin Péret, Remedios Varo, Victor Brauner, Max Ernst, Lam, Jean Malaquais, and Vlady. See "'Au Brûleur de Loups', André Breton, Anna Seghers, Jean Malaquais" at http://www.galerie-alain-paire.com.

Figueres . . . Castelldefels . . . the International Brigades: Organized by the Comintern during the Spanish Civil War, the International Brigades fought against Franco in defense of the Spanish Republic but also against the anarchists and the Partido Obrero de Unificación Marxista, of which Serge was a supporter. (In *Homage to Catalonia*, George Orwell chronicles his own experiences in the POUM militia.) In "Espagne," 25 mars 1941, *Carnets*, 57–58, Serge describes Figueres and Castelldefels from the sea:

> Seven o'clock in the morning, weak sunlight, we are leaving behind the cloudy, snow-covered Pyrenees. Green plain of Figueres, how many dead under that grass. Figueres of the defeat, a gentle, calm landscape, green hills. Small Catalan towns at the water's edge. The coast drifts by like a dream, real and unreal. High verdant hills, castles on the hilltops. —A great, square castle made of red brick, flanked by a gray outer wall lying upon the slope, Castelldefels. A former POUM militiaman, who is just bones and nerves, with the hard face of a sick miner (concentration camps in Germany, then Spanish battle fronts, prisons, camps again in Spain and France), explains that this was the prison and torture site of the International Brigades. It's probably one of Franco's prisons now.

Caribbean Sea, p. 103

Published in *Lettres françaises*, no. 4 (Buenos Aires, 1 April 1942): 18–19. (JR)

voracious sea, dangerous sea: In "Les vagues – Mer redoutable," 16 juin 1941, *Carnets*, 101, Serge describes at length the spectacle of Caribbean waves striking the shore with the sound of a "distant cannonade," concluding:

> This assault never stops . . . I've already seen many waves, why am I so struck by the powerful rage of these, by their nasty hissing, by their continuous destructive surge? Because here I feel the destructive surge, this hot sea of the Caribs is not a

gentle Mediterranean, it is something else, something danger-
ously unstable. Fearsome sea.

Our Children, p. 105
Published in *Le Journal des Poètes*, no. 1 (Brussels, 1958): 10. (JR)

Death of Jacques Mesnil, p. 106
Jacques Mesnil (1872–1940) was the author of studies on Masaccio and
Botticelli and a fast friend of Serge's. He and his wife Clara Koettlitz
were former students of Élisée Reclus (1830–1905), the anarchist geog-
rapher and a veteran of the Paris Commune. "Toward the age of fifty,
Clara lost her reason; Jacques died alone in 1940," fleeing the Nazis
during the fall of France (*Memoirs*, 166–167).
the Pré-Saint-Gervais: Serge lived in this Paris neighborhood from
mid-May 1937 to mid-June 1940. (JR)

Altagracia, p. 109
Altagracia: The name evokes the Virgen de la Altagracia, spiritual
protector of the Dominican Republic (Christopher Winks, private
communication).

In a long, untitled entry dated fin juillet 1941, *Carnets*, 104–105,
Serge describes the scene, characters, and events that find a different
expression in the poem:

> Little cemetery crowded with cement crosses out my
> window . . . Last night, awakened by the storm, saw this cem-
> etery all spread out, very beautiful, as if at an oblique angle
> with all its crosses bent beneath the unending bolts of light-
> ning—of a dazzling, immobile whiteness—and the living
> spears of relentless rain. On an upright gray cross I can read:
> Porfirio Kepi . . .
>
> Three Chinese, with children, often come to visit a new
> grave . . .
>
> Several days in a row, a poor woman returned . . . Thirty
> maybe, already wrinkled, very thin, the body of a slender
> young girl . . . Dressed all in black, with a little hat and her
> stockings pulled up, she looks like an insect. Under the hard
> brilliant sun she arrives with a little black purse, a black
> umbrella. She brings flowers, a candle, tidies up the gravestone,
> removes the dead flowers, picks up a scrap of paper and takes
> it away, sits down for moment on a burning white gravestone,
> folds her hands, waits . . . She was alone in all this whiteness
> of crosses, under this awful sun, I saw her talking to the cross,

with discouraged gestures: No, really, I can't believe it, how is that possible? . . . She saw me, I was embarrassed.

Mexico: Idyll, p. 111

Published in *Contemporains/revue de critique et de littérature*, no. 4 (Paris, April 1951): 501–502. (JR)

Marcel Martinet (1887–1944), a close friend of Serge's, was a poet, playwright, novelist, and critic, as well as an antifascist and anti-Stalin activist. Martinet had, like his friend Mesnil, a rare force of character and moral and ideological rigor. (JR) See Paizis, *Marcel Martinet*.

Mexico: Morning Litany, p. 113

Published in Spanish as "Letanía de la mañana," Oscar Vera, trans., in *Revue Babel/Revista de Arte y Crítica* III, no. 33 (Santiago de Chile/ Buenos Aires/Mexico City, May–June 1946): 104–105. (JR)

Flammenwerfer: Flamethrowers.

A las dos y a las tres: In "Virgen de Guadalupe," 11–12 décembre 1943, *Carnets*, 415–420, Serge recounts a visit to the Basilica de Santa María de Guadalupe with Laurette Séjourné. In the crowd at a festival they watch a group of pilgrims singing over and over again a litany like the fragment in the poem: "a la una y a las dos / a las tres y a las cuatro / a las cinco y a las seis / dieron gracias por el alma . . ." (at one o'clock and two / at three o'clock and four / at five o'clock and six / they gave thanks for the soul . . .).

Mexico: Churches, p. 115

In 1943 and 1944, Serge made pilgrimages to the newly formed Paricutín volcano near San Juan Parangaricutiro. During the first visit, in August 1943, Serge witnessed the Indios engaged in an otherworldly rite:

> High, broad nave of the church, very poor. A group of the faithful is performing its devotions there. They are standing up, opposite the choir. The church is filled with a gently rhythmical, furtive sound. From deep inside, the unshod faithful slowly retreat toward the exit as they perform a sort of dance in place. The silhouettes of men in sarapes and of women carrying their kids wrapped in a shawl on their chests hop straight up, take a quick half-step forward, a small step back . . . It's a long, magical dance in the Christian church. An old woman comes in and advances toward the altar, on her knees . . . These people are sunbrowned, thin, and impoverished, with tense faces, with solemn, deep-set eyes. They dance slowly past us, not deigning to see us . . .

An Indio is sweeping the ash-covered parvis. The immense
slanting cloud of Paricutín covers half the noon sky. ("Dr Atl,"
[22 août 1943], *Carnets*, 392–393)

the Trinity Lavra of Saint Sergius: A venerable Russian Orthodox mon-
astery in the town of Sergiyev Posad, not far from Moscow.

Outbreaks, p. 118
Père Ubu: The usurping regicide protagonist of Alfred Jarry's play *Ubu
Roi* (King Ubu).

We have long thought . . ., p. 122
A version of the lines "the habit of still believing / more in the earth
than in the grave" serves as an epigraph to part III of Serge's last novel,
Unforgiving Years, Richard Greeman, trans. (New York: New York
Review Books, 2008).

Note, p. 123
A version of the last stanza serves as an epigraph to part I of *Unforgiving
Years*.

It takes . . ., p. 124
A version of the last stanza serves as an epigraph to part IV of
Unforgiving Years.

After that splendid Notre Dame . . ., p. 125
Published in *Le Journal des Poètes*, no. 1 (Brussels, 1958): 10. Also in
Resistance, as "Sensation." (JR)

It's salt water that quenches . . ., p. 126
Published in *Contemporains*, no. 4 (Paris, April 1951): 499–500. (JR) A
version of the lines "All the cities I have known, all the unknown cities
/ drift, cracked ice floes, toward the most barren dawns" serves as an
epigraph to part II of *Unforgiving Years*.

III. Mains/Hands
Published in a special issue of *Témoins*, no. 21 (Zurich, February 1959):
31–33; published in Spanish as "Manos" in *Presencia/Revista ecuatoriana
de cultura*, nos. 7–8 (Quito, August–September 1950). Thanks to Vlady,
the poem was published in a bilingual, fine-press edition, with a Spanish
translation by the poet Verónica Volkow: *Mains/Manos: Un Poema de
Victor Serge* (Mexico: Carta al Lector y El Taller Martín Pescador, 1978);
the edition includes an engraving from Vlady's sketch of his father's
hands. (JR) That sketch is reproduced on the cover of this translation.

Serge's last poem, written the day before his death in November 1947, has parallels with Rimbaud's "Les mains de Jeanne-Marie," as Renée Morel suggests in a private communication. As translated by Paul Schmidt, Rimbaud's poem, with its Communard heroine, begins: "Jeanne-Marie has powerful hands, / Dark hands summertime has tanned, / Hands pale as a dead man's hands" ("The Hands of Jeanne-Marie," in *Arthur Rimbaud: Complete Works* [New York: Harper & Row, 1976], 57). In his edition of Rimbaud's poems, Jean-Luc Steinmetz links "Jeanne-Marie" to Rimbaud's reading of Théophile Gautier's "Études de mains" (Hand Studies) (*Poésies* [Paris: Flammarion, 2004], 256). The first part of Gautier's poem interrogates the sculpture of a beautiful woman's hand; the second part describes the severed hand of the criminal dandy Lacenaire after his execution. Serge was likely familiar with Rimbaud's poem and possibly with Gautier's.

See Richard Greeman, "Afterword: The Odyssey of a Revolutionary Poet" in this book for Vlady's note on his father's last hours.

Afterword: The Odyssey of a Revolutionary Poet

Richard Greeman

Victor Serge was born Victor Lvovich Kibalchich in 1890 in Brussels, where his parents, impoverished Russian anti-czarist intellectuals in exile, had settled in their perennial "quest of their daily bread and of good libraries." Serge was homeschooled by his impecunious father, Leon Kibalchich, whose overwhelming passion for science left him unsuited for things practical, and by his mother Vera Poderevskaya, a former teacher who taught him to read through "cheap editions of Shakespeare and Chekov."[1] Young Serge was thus spared the dispiriting boredom of institutional schooling while learning how to think for himself, love poetry, and pursue science out of passionate curiosity.

Serge's nuclear family broke up when he was fifteen; his mother, suffering from tuberculosis, returned to Russia. Serge chose to live alone in Brussels, where he had bonded with a band of other youths: underpaid teenage apprentices, all passionate readers, thirsting for absolutes, and "closer than brothers." Together, Serge and his companions began their political education as activists in the Socialist Young Guards of the Belgian Workers' Party. But they soon lost patience with turn-of-the-century reformism and formed their own militant anarchist group, which published a paper,

---

Richard Greeman is the translator of five of Victor Serge's seven novels: *Men in Prison*, *Birth of Our Power*, *Conquered City*, *Midnight in the Century*, and *Unforgiving Years*. He has published literary, political, and biographical studies of Serge in English, French, Russian, and Spanish, as well as prefaces to French editions of Serge's books.

Le Révolté (The Rebel), in which Serge signed his articles "Le Rétif" (The Maverick). Poetry held a special place in the early twentieth-century revolutionary movements in which Serge evolved. As he later recalled:

> Poetry was a substitute for prayer for us, so greatly did it uplift us and answer our constant need for exaltation. Verhaeren, the European poet nearest to Walt Whitman (whom we did not yet know), flashed us a gleam of keen, anguished, fertile thought on the modern town, its railway stations, its trade in women, its swirling crowds, and his cries of violence were like ours: "*Open or break your fists against the door!*" Fists were broken, and why not? Better that than stagnation. Jehan Rictus lamented the suffering of the penniless intellectual dragging out his nights on the benches of foreign boulevards, and no rhymes were richer than his: *songe-mensonge* (dream-lie), *espoir-désespoir* (hope-despair). In springtime "*the smell of crap and lilacs . . .*"[2]

If Serge remembers such rhymes and phrases from Rictus, it is perhaps because they so accurately reflect the mood of his youth. In December 1908, on the eve of his eighteenth birthday, Le Rétif poured his own despair into a long article on Rictus, in whose poetry he saw "poverty symbolized, incarnated, gifted with language . . . a marvelous language full of unexpected figures—vulgar, naïve, even burlesque but of such penetrating poetry!"[3]

Serge and his Brussels comrades, although too poor to go to school, were nonetheless great readers. Through the Workers' Party, in whose cultural activities the Belgian Symbolist poets and playwrights Verhaeren and Maeterlinck were intensely involved, they were exposed to avant-garde writers, musicians, and painters. And they were regulars at the party's Maison du Peuple, which organized discussions on subjects like modern Russian literature, Ibsen, Wagner, Shakespeare, William Morris, and Verlaine.

Fin-de-siècle Europe was marked by the high tide of Symbolist poetry, which coincided with the high tide of bomb-throwing anarchism. For several years, the two movements carried on a curious flirtation. Thus we find names like Paul Valéry, Stéphane Mallarmé, and Émile Verhaeren alongside the names of radicals like Félix Fénéon, Lucien Descaves, Charles Malato, Saint-Pol-Roux, and Octave Mirbeau in the pages of anarchist reviews like Jean Grave's *Le Révolté* and Zo d'Axa's *L'En-dehors*. The period's aesthetic is epitomized by a notorious remark by the anarchist poet Laurent Tailhade at a banquet attended by Verlaine, Mallarmé, Rodin, and Zola. Asked his opinion of Auguste Vaillant's bombing of the Chamber of Deputies in 1893, Tailhade replied, "What matter the victims if the gesture be beautiful?" In this atmosphere, Serge and his fellow teenage agitators felt no contradiction between their love of poetry and their increasingly violent anarchist militancy.

By 1909 Serge and his friends had drifted over to Paris, where they became individualist anarchists. One of the tenets of individualist anarchism was "illegalism": the right of "individual expropriation," that is, theft. A rift developed in the group between the ruthlessly Spencerian "scientifics" and the "sentimentals." Among the latter were Serge; his first great love, Rirette Maîtrejean; and his closest Paris friend, René Valet, with whom he spent long nights pacing the Latin Quarter reciting and discussing poetry: "Together we muttered scraps of Vildrac's *White Bird*, Jules Romains's *Ode to the Crowd*, Jehan Rictus's *The Ghost*."[4] Nonetheless, this heady mixture of solidarity, idealism, and illegalist doctrine, combined with poverty and despair, led inexorably to tragedy. By 1913 Valet and most of Serge's companions had perished on the guillotine or in shoot-outs with the police in their doomed war against an opulent, complacent society.

Serge did not participate in the bloody bank robberies of the "tragic bandits of French anarchy" (aka the Bonnot Gang), but he refused to testify against them, and he glorified their deeds in his weekly paper *l'anarchie* until he himself was arrested. At the trial in 1913, Serge and Maîtrejean were in the dock with the surviving bandits, who were sentenced to die on the guillotine or to life terms on Devil's Island. Maîtrejean got off with time served, but Serge was condemned to five years in the penitentiary (1912–1917). (This ordeal inspired his first novel, *Men in Prison* [1930].)[5] He survived thanks to mental self-discipline, physical exercise, "and recourse to that exaltation, or light spiritual intoxication, which is provided by great works of poetry. Altogether, [he] spent around fifteen months in solitary confinement, in various conditions, some of them quite hellish."[6] Nonetheless, the poems "Un jour de pluie" (A Rainy Day) and "Je sais des plaines" (I Know Plains), perhaps smuggled out of prison, appeared in an individualist-anarchist review in the middle of the First World War.

Expelled from France in 1917, Serge spent six months in Barcelona, where he worked as a typesetter, wrote for the anarcho-syndicalist press, and participated in a failed uprising of the workers. (It was in this period that he started using the name Victor Serge.) Serge chronicled the people and events in his novel *Birth of Our Power* (1931),[7] and he recorded his impressions in *Notations d'Espagne* (1917), a series of prose poems.

Serge and Soviet Literature

As the revolution in Barcelona sputtered, Serge set out to join the ascending revolution in Russia. This perilous journey entailed crossing Europe in the middle of the war. Serge had been forbidden to reenter France after his expulsion, but reenter he did, only to find himself locked up as a Bolshevik suspect in a French concentration camp, desperate and without papers. Finally, after the Armistice, Serge and other Russians were exchanged as hostages against French officers held in Soviet Russia. He arrived in Petrograd in January 1919 to find not a great turbulent revolutionary forum but a grim, frozen, starving, besieged city struggling to survive under the iron discipline of the Communist Party, a situation that Serge explores in *Conquered City* (1932).[8]

Although Serge's spoken Russian was rusty at first, he had long-standing connections with the Russian poetry of his time. As early as 1909, we find him eking out a precarious living in Paris translating Russian novels and the poetry of Artsybashev, Balmont, and Merezhkovsky. Later in Paris, while attempting to cross into Russia to join the revolutionaries, he struck up a friendship with the Acmeist poet Nikolai Stepanovich Gumilev, who was on his way to join the Whites. "I am a traditionalist, monarchist, imperialist, and pan-Slavist," declared Gumilev. "Mine is the true Russian nature, just as it was formed by Orthodox Christianity. You also have the true Russian nature, but at its opposite extreme, that of spontaneous anarchy, primitive violence, and unruly belief. I love all of Russia, even what I want to fight in it, even what you represent."[9] In 1921 Serge, by then an influential Communist, was to struggle in vain to stop the Cheka from shooting this friend and adversary whose face and poems were to haunt him for years.

Among the first people Serge saw on arriving in Petrograd was Maxim Gorky, a relation of Serge's mother's family, who was at that time bitterly critical of the Bolshevik's dictatorial methods. Gorky offered Serge a position in his international publishing house, but Serge, despite similar misgivings about the authoritarianism of the Bolsheviks, could not stand on the sidelines and threw himself body and soul into the defense of the revolution. He joined the militia, went to work for the press services of the Communist International, and ultimately joined the Party, all the while retaining his anarchist reservations about Communist authoritarianism.

One of the factors that won Serge over to the Communists was their support of the arts. In besieged Petrograd the unheated theaters and concert halls were full to the rafters with roughly dressed men and women, while poets were declaiming in cafés and on street corners and public spaces were given over to avant-garde artists to decorate. Trotsky, the Commissar of War, was writing literary criticism on his armored train at the same time that Viktor Shklovsky was writing his seminal *Theory of Prose* and serving as instructor and political commissar in an armored car unit.

From the time of his arrival in revolutionary Russia, Serge was in contact with poets and writers. The articles on Soviet literary life he penned for the French magazine *Clarté* in the 1920s provide fascinating portraits of poets like Alexander Blok, Andrei Bely, Sergei Yesenin, Osip Mandelstam, Boris Pasternak, and Vladimir Mayakovsky, as well as penetrating analyses and appreciations of their work.[10]

According to Serge, most of the poets of the prewar Silver Age had a conciliatory attitude toward the revolution. The epic spirit of the revolution, he wrote in 1922, had sparked new creative impulses among the poets, whether of Christian, Symbolist, or Futurist inspiration. Citing the examples of Bely's "Christ Is Risen" (which Serge translated into French), of Blok's mystical vision of Christ marching in a snowstorm at the head of a band of Red Guards in "The Twelve," and of Mayakovsky's grandiose "One Hundred and Fifty Million," Serge concludes: "The fact is that there is a profound lyricism in the revolution, that it is a new faith, and that at all times it teaches us to sacrifice the old, shrinking, outworn and outdated values for new values . . . it sometimes arouses an irresistible sense of greatness in the individual."[11] Serge's own poems of the period—including "Mitrailleuse" (Machine Gun, 1919), "La flamme sur la neige" (The Flame upon the Snow, 1920–21), "Ville" (City, 1920), and "Max" (1921)—were infused with this epic mood.

Yet Serge's accounts of these pro-Soviet poets are also tinged with increasing anguish as he witnesses the gradual extinction of the creative outpouring of this heroic period under the pressures of conformity, falseness, and corruption. "What can I do now in this life?" Bely asked him despondently one evening. "I cannot live outside this Russia of ours and I cannot breathe within it."[12]

Serge had viewed the Red Terror during the Civil War as an unavoidable necessity, while protesting against its excesses. However, he considered its perpetuation into the succeeding period of relative calm (the New Economic Policy of the post–Civil War period) to be "an immense and demoralizing blunder."[13] Serge believed that opening free markets while repressing political freedom could only lead to corruption, and he saw "the gigantic scale of certain royalties"[14] during the NEP as a corrupting influence encouraging the worst kind of official literary conformity.

By the mid-1920s Serge found himself surrounded by suicides: first, among idealistic Communist militants protesting the stifling of inner-Party debate, driven to despair by pervasive bureaucratization and corruption, and then among the poets: "The telephone rings: 'Come quickly, Yesenin has killed himself.' I run out in the snow, I enter his room in the Hotel International, and I can hardly recognize him; he no longer looks himself," Serge recalls.[15] Yesenin "had tried to be in tune with the times, and with our official literature," Serge remarks of this flamboyant, decadent Bohemian. But soon Yesenin found himself despairing: "'I am a stranger in my own land . . .'; 'My poems are no longer needed now, and I myself am unwanted . . .'; . . . 'I am not a new man, I have one foot in the past, and yet I wish, I the stumbler, I the cripple, to join the cohorts of steel once more . . .'"[16]

Mayakovsky, a Party member who was himself soon to commit suicide, had addressed a reproachful farewell to Yesenin that depicts the poet circling in the void and "hustling the stars." Serge describes how in public readings "Mayakovsky . . . coiled like a spring in a bantering style of violence, hammered out his farewell before audiences for whom [Yesenin's] death was turning into a symbol:

This planet's not well equipped for happiness;
Happiness will only be won at a future date!"[17]

The advent of the Stalinist repression in 1928–1929 and the rise of the doctrine of socialist realism in 1932 spelled the doom of originality and independence in the arts. In "The Writer's Conscience," published shortly before his death in 1947,[18] Serge recalls a literary soirée at the home of Osip Mandelstam in 1932, during which the poet read aloud a recently completed nature poem and asked his friends if they thought it was "publishable." Mandelstam was trying to write "safe" poetry, but the voice of freedom within him was so strong that he could not censor it. For Serge, Mandelstam's "visions of the lake of Erivan and of the snows of Ararat raised in the murmur of a breeze a demand for liberty, a subversive praise of the imagination, an affirmation of ungovernable thought."[19]

A few months after the evening with Mandelstam, Serge was arrested, interrogated for months in the Lubianka, a notorious secret prison, and deported to Orenburg in the Urals. Within months Mandelstam was also arrested; he apparently died in the camps. If Serge survived, it was thanks to a vigorous campaign for his freedom led by left-wing writers and a teachers' union in France. But Serge's case was a rare exception. For the most part, pro-Soviet writers and intellectuals in the West remained silent throughout an entire decade during which writers like Mandelstam, Boris Pilnyak, and Isaac Babel—personally known to them and translated into every language—were massacred. "No PEN club, even those who had offered them banquets, posed the least question on their cases," Serge writes, decrying their "universal complicity."[20]

Also in "The Writer's Conscience," Serge praised the courage of the poets of the French Resistance, including Louis Aragon and Paul Éluard (former Surrealists who had become Stalinists), while also praising Jean-Paul Sartre's concept of committed literature. However, Serge could not hide his indignation at the collaboration of the poets with another totalitarianism, Soviet Communism: "But that such [anti-Nazi] poetry should often be signed by poets who elsewhere praise the hangman, praise the torturer, insult the shot, speak untruths over the tombs of another Resistance inspired by the same motives—the defense of man against tyranny—that leads us, by a terrible alchemy, to the negation of all affirmed values."[21]

Resistance

Serge wrote the bulk of the poems in *Resistance* (1938) while in deportation in Orenburg in 1933–1936. When he arrived the once-prosperous provincial capital of the Kazakhs (or Kirghiz), a nomadic people of the steppes of Central Asia, was in the throes of famine. Serge was joined by his son Vlady and his wife Liuba Russakova, who had been hospitalized in Leningrad for schizophrenia (triggered by political persecution). In the beginning Liuba's symptoms were in remission in Orenburg, but soon her violent crises returned, and she had to be returned to the hospital in Moscow. ("Tête-à-Tête" is an imaginary dialogue with her.) Vlady, already a budding artist, remained with Serge, and from that time on he accompanied his father from deportation to exile until Serge's death in Mexico in 1947.

In deportation, gainful employment was out of the question as long as Serge refused to toe the Party line, and the struggle for bread and firewood was a daily preoccupation. When the GPU cut off Serge's correspondence with France (the source of his meager royalties), the family nearly starved. About this period Serge writes:

> I was finishing my books in a state of uncertainty. What would their destiny be, and mine? . . . By one of those strokes of irony that are so frequent in Russia, the Soviet press was, quite appropriately, commemorating an anniversary of the Ukrainian national poet Taras Shevchenko, who in 1847 had been exiled for ten years to the steppes of Orenburg, "forbidden to draw or to write." He did, all the same, write some clandestine poetry that he concealed in his boots. In

> this report I had an overwhelming insight into the
> persistence in our Russian land, after a century of
> reform, progress, and revolution, of the same willful
> determination to wipe out the rebellious intelligence
> without mercy. Never mind, I told myself, I must hold
> on: hold on and work on, even under this slab of lead.[22]

Serge's determination is evident in such poems as "Be Hard," "Trust," and "Stenka Razin." But the overwhelming feeling in the Orenburg poems is one of fraternity: of identity and communion with the land, with its people, and ultimately with the universe itself. For Serge, "he who speaks, he who writes is essentially someone speaking for all those who are voiceless"[23]—those memorialized in "People of the Ural," "Old Woman," "The Asphyxiated Man," and "Constellation of Dead Brothers," for example.

Serge joined a clandestine cell of Oppositionists in Orenburg. Some were Old Bolsheviks who had fought in the revolutions of 1905 and 1917; others, like Serge, had joined the Party during the Civil War. All were distinguished by the courage and integrity that had brought them, by a tragic irony of history, from the summits of a power wrested from the hands of czarist reaction back to the status of persecuted, exiled, and imprisoned rebels. All were to perish resisting. "I have described these men," writes Serge, "because I am grateful to them for having existed, and because they incarnated an epoch."[24] It is to them that *Resistance* is dedicated.

On the other hand, during Stalin's bloody show trials (which began in the summer of 1936, just a few months after Serge was released from Russia), a number of Old Bolsheviks reviled themselves and confessed to trumped-up charges out of fear, Party loyalty, or despair. In "Confessions" Serge portrays their inner drama, perhaps more intimately than does Arthur Koestler in *Darkness at Noon*.

Serge fictionalizes his Oppositionist comrades in *Midnight in the Century* (1939),[25] which is based largely on his

Orenburg experience. Vlady told me that the "comrades" often held their secret political meetings out of doors, under the cover of country excursions, for example, going by rowboat to the forest on the other side of the Ural from Orenburg. "Boat on the Ural" meditates on one such excursion.

Messages

In July 1935 the fellow-traveling writer Romain Rolland visited Stalin in the Kremlin and extracted his promise to release Serge and allow him to move abroad with his family. Yet Serge was to remain in captivity until April 1936 because no democratic country would take him in. Trotsky, whom Stalin had expelled from Russia in 1928, had faced the same dilemma: both men inhabited a "planet without visas."[26] Finally, thanks to the intervention of the writer Charles Plisnier and of Emile Vandervelde, a former prime minister of Belgium, Serge was granted temporary residency in Brussels. Serge did not reach Paris, the center of publishing and political life, for yet another year, because the French still considered him a dangerous anarchist subject to a 1917 expulsion order.

Only three months after Serge's return to Europe, Franco launched his coup against the Spanish Republic and Stalin began liquidating the Bolsheviks of Lenin's generation at the Moscow Trials. From then on, the struggle against totalitarianism occupied Serge's energies, and literature had to take a back seat.[27] We thus have only two poems from Paris, and it was not until 1939 that Serge, his "militant's duty done" (as he wrote to a friend) devoted himself to the novel *Midnight in the Century*.

In 1936, on the eve of André Gide's voyage to the Soviet Union, Serge wrote Gide an open letter warning him to look behind the scenes and daring him to publish the truth of what he would find there. [28] Gide did precisely that, and the publication of *Return from the U.S.S.R.* earned him the enmity of Moscow and of French Stalinists and fellow travelers like

Aragon. Gide also journeyed to Brussels to meet with Serge before publishing his *Afterthoughts on the U.S.S.R.*, where his criticism of Stalinism was sharper and more systematic.

Also in 1936, with the Surrealist poet André Breton and others (such as Marcel Martinet, the poet to whom "Mexico: Idyll" is dedicated), Serge formed the Committee for Inquiry into the Moscow Trials and the Defense of Free Speech in the Revolution. Serge foresaw that Stalin would extend his purges into civil war Spain and the need to defend independent revolutionaries there. The Committee soon had its hands full when the Spanish Communists engineered the suppression of a rival, anti-Stalinist Marxist party, the Partido Obrero de Unificación Marxista (POUM), to which Serge was an adviser, and kidnapped its leader, Serge's close friend Andrés Nin.

Between 1936 and 1939, Serge produced a stream of pamphlets, books, and articles revealing the truth about Stalinism, but he was boycotted by the mainstream press, dominated by the Popular Front antifascist alliance with the Communists. Ironically, Serge ended up working as a proofreader for Socialist newspapers that would not print his authentic explanations of the mystery of the Moscow Trials. His other source of income was the weekly column he wrote for the independent, union-backed daily paper, *La Wallonie* of Liège, Belgium, in which he commented on history, culture, politics, and world events in the run-up to war.[29] Beholden to no one and to no party, Serge offered a unique perspective on a crucial period that stretched from the euphoria of the Communist-Socialist alliance of the Popular Front to the eve of France's defeat in the Second World War.

Serge placed the two poems he wrote in Paris, "Sunday" (1939) and "After that splendid Notre Dame . . ." (1938), first and next to last in *Messages* (1946).[30] Both poems are dedicated to his companion, Laurette Séjourné. And both poems render the uncanny atmosphere of Paris on the eve of war, which Serge describes so vividly in *Unforgiving Years*.[31] In "After that splendid Notre Dame," "the wide-awake sleeper" experiences a vision of transcendence and connection as he follows the eternally recurring "hope-filled cortege of his executed brothers" along the quays of the Seine. In "Sunday" Serge portrays a ragged café beggar who is a reincarnation of Rictus's monologist, now transmogrified into "a corpse in a fedora" in an Apocalypse "completely devoid of interest" to the patrons of the café.

After the French military collapsed before the Nazi onslaught, Serge left Paris at the very last moment, as enemy tanks were penetrating the town. He, Laurette, Vlady, and a Spanish friend joined the exodus on foot, eventually arriving in Marseille, where, along with hundreds of antifascist refugees trapped in Vichy France, they haunted the prefecture and the consulates in a relentless search for exit permits and visas. Serge depicts the haunted atmosphere of that time and place in *The Long Dusk* (1946).[32]

In Marseille Serge worked closely with Varian Fry of the Emergency Rescue Committee to vet and aid antifascist refugees. When Fry and his coworkers rented a big, ramshackle villa just outside of town, they invited Serge, Vlady, and Laurette to move in. Serge dubbed the place "Villa Espervisa" and suggested inviting Breton and his family to join them. Before long, the villa was hosting guests like Victor Brauner, Jacques Hérold, Wifredo Lam, André Masson, Benjamin Péret, and Remedios Varo for regular Surrealist activities.[33] In the library of the Villa Air-Bel, Serge would work on his novel of the Stalinist purges, *The Case of Comrade Tulayev*,[34] while Breton wrote "poems in the greenhouse."[35]

Although Breton rejected Serge's realistic political fiction as passé, Serge joined in Surrealist games with Breton and his friends, while remaining critical of Surrealism and certain Surrealists. For example, during their transatlantic journey, Serge privately expressed dismay that Breton, who practiced astrology, proved ignorant of the first elements of astronomy under the night sky.[36] ("Out at Sea," the love poem Serge composed during that voyage on an old wreck of a freighter overcrowded with refugees, is dedicated to Laurette, who remained in France, joining Serge in Mexico a year later.)

When the *Capitaine Paul-Lemerle* arrived in Martinique, the Vichy French officials interned Serge and Vlady in a former quarantine barracks with other refugees. There Vlady sketched his father calmly seated at his typewriter and writing; perhaps Serge is working on "The rats are leaving . . ." with its dystopian vision of the planet as refugee ship to which we must hold on "with a bitter grip / As one clings to floating hulks" and with its final, sanguinary call for justice.

Serge and Vlady were eventually granted temporary residency in Ciudad Trujillo, Dominican Republic, where in April 1941 Serge quickly wrote a short book on Germany's invasion of Russia, *Hitler contra Stalin*.[37] Serge also wrote two poems included in *Messages*, "Altagracia" and "Caribbean Sea."

Thanks to a campaign by supporters like Dwight and Nancy Macdonald in New York and exiled Spanish comrades like Julián Gorkin in Mexico City, President Lázaro Cárdenas of Mexico offered Serge asylum. He arrived in Mexico a year after the assassination of Trotsky, only to find himself the object of Communist slander campaigns in the press ("fascist agent"), leading up to an armed Stalinist attack when Serge tried to speak in a public meeting. (Serge escaped, but several of his comrades were hospitalized.)

As for Mexico itself, Serge instantly fell in love with the country. And it was in Mexico that wrote most of the poems of *Messages* and finished his greatest prose works: *Memoirs of a Revolutionary* and the novels *The Case of Comrade Tulayev* and *Unforgiving Years*, all unpublished at his death. He immersed himself in Mexican archaeology, geography, geology, and culture, eventually writing a short book on pre-Columbian civilization, a subject that Laurette Séjourné, later known as an archaeologist, was studying at the university.[38] Everywhere he saw similarities between the peoples and landscapes of Mexico and those of Russia and Central Asia.

As Serge records in his *Memoirs*, he was enchanted by Mexico from his first glimpse of the country through the window of the DC-3 that brought him and Vlady from Ciudad Trujillo:

> The airplane instructs us in a new vision of the world whose lyrical richness could provide material for a renewed art form to flourish, whether in poetry or painting. But this semi-bankrupt civilization has made it into a killing machine; it is used for travel only by the rich, who are dead to any kind of enthusiasm. We see them dozing in the comfortable seats of the Douglas aircraft, and all the while we are winging over the Caribbean Sea, the storm-ridden lands of Yucatan, and then the tablelands of Mexico, covered in heavy clouds which are transfixed by shafts of light. Huge, rose-pink, and solid, Tenayuca's Pyramid of the Sun stands out suddenly on its flinty plain.[39]

The theoretician of that new art form based on the aerial vision was the painter Gerardo Murillo, who called himself Dr. Atl. Dr. Atl was a notorious political renegade whom Serge encountered during his trips to the Paricutín volcano, which had sprung up in a farmer's field in 1943.

Serge's experiences of the volcano's vast destructive powers, as well as of Mexico's earthquakes, had a powerful effect on his imagination, which is evident in the Mexican poems as well as in *Unforgiving Years*, whose final section is set in Mexico. For Serge, geological revolutions were a natural metaphor for the human revolutions and catastrophes of totalitarianism and the apocalypse of total industrial war on a planetary scale. Serge used the word "pandestruction" to describe the massive, mechanized hyperviolence of the Second World War.

Serge's wartime poems abound in images of radical destruction, as in "Altagracia," in which nature's violence is indistinguishable from the violence of war in the dream vision of a cemetery in a tropical storm: "Its battalion of crosses seemed to start moving. / A host of eyeless faces were revealed in the slanting mirrors of lightning bolts, / All the world's mirrors were breaking at once, sweeping away the disfigured faces of armies." More than half a century later, Serge's cataclysmic evocations have a contemporary ring, prophetic of our era of acid rain, overheated atmosphere, melting ice floes, rising oceans, floods, droughts, and cyclones: pandestruction magnified to a truly planetary scale.

"Hands"

The magnificent elegy "Hands," with its intimations of mortality, was the last poem, the last words, that Serge was to write. Vlady tells the story:[40]

> One day in November of 1947 my father brought a poem to my house in Mexico City. Not finding me at home, he left to take a walk downtown. From the central post office, he mailed me the poem. A short while later, he died in a taxi. That night a friend came to bring me the news. I found him on an operating table in the police station. A yellowish lamp illuminated the sinister room. The first thing I noticed were his shoes: they had holes in them. This shocked me, for he was careful about his dress, although his clothes were always of the cheapest. The following day, I was unable to draw his face, for they had put a plaster death-mask over it. I limited myself to drawing his hands, which were beautiful. A few days later, I received his poem: "Hands."

Notes

1   Victor Serge, *Memoirs of a Revolutionary*, Peter Sedgwick with George Paizis, trans. (New York: New York Review Books, 2012), 5.
2   Ibid., 21.
3   Le Rétif, "Jehan Rictus: Les soliloques du pauvre" (décembre 1908), published posthumously by Émile Armand in *L'Unique*, no. 36 (janvier–février 1949).

4   Serge, *Memoirs,* 63.

5   Victor Serge, *Men in Prison,* Richard Greeman, trans. (Oakland, CA: PM Press, 2014).

6   Serge, *Memoirs,* 44.

7   Victor Serge, *Birth of Our Power,* Richard Greeman, trans. (Oakland, CA: PM Press, 2014).

8   Victor Serge, *Conquered City,* Richard Greeman, trans. (New York: New York Review Books, 2011).

9   Serge, *Memoirs,* 69.

10 See Victor Serge, *Collected Writings on Literature and Revolution,* Al Richardson, trans. and ed. (London: Francis Boutle, 2004).

11 Serge, *Literature and Revolution,* 153–155.

12 Serge, *Memoirs,* 179.

13 Ibid., 179.

14 Ibid., 236.

15 Ibid., 229

16 Ibid., 230.

17 Ibid., 230.

18 Victor Serge, "The Writer's Conscience," in David Craig, ed., *Marxists on Literature: An Anthology* (Harmondsworth: Penguin Books, 1975), 435–444.

19 Ibid., 437.

20 Ibid., 440.

21 Ibid., 442.

22 Ibid., 368.

23 Ibid., 53.

24 Ibid., 361.

25 Victor Serge, *Midnight in the Century,* Richard Greeman, trans. (New York: New York Review Books, 2015).

26 Trotsky used the phrase as the title of a chapter in his autobiography, the phrase occurs in the first line of "Marseille," and Jean Malaquais borrowed the phrase for the title of his Marseille novel.

27 Serge's *From Lenin to Stalin* and *Russia Twenty Years After* are available in English translation.

28 Serge, *Memoirs,* 390–391. For Mitchell Abidor's translation of "Open Letter to André Gide," see https://www.marxists.org/archive/serge/1936/xx/letter-gide.htm.

29 For a selection of these articles, see Victor Serge, *Retour à l'Ouest: Chroniques (juin 1936–mai 1940),* textes choisis et annotés par Anthony Glinoer, préface de Richard Greeman (Marseille: Agone, 2010).

30 Nineteen forty-six is the date of completion of the *Messages* manuscript, not the date of publication. Its first publication is in Victor Serge, *Pour un brasier dans un désert* (Bassac [Charente], France:

Plein Chant, 1998), thanks to the efforts of the editor of that collection, Jean Rière.

31 Victor Serge, *Unforgiving Years*, Richard Greeman, trans. (New York: New York Review Books, 2008).

32 Victor Serge, *The Long Dusk*, Ralph Manheim, trans. (New York: Dial Press, 1946). The original French title *Les Derniers temps* (End Times) is more apocalyptic.

33 See Rosemary Sullivan, *Villa Air-Bel: World War II, Escape, and a House in Marseille* (New York: HarperCollins, 2006).

34 Victor Serge, *The Case of Comrade Tulayev*, Willard R. Trask, trans. (New York: New York Review Books, 2004).

35 Serge, *Memoirs*, 426.

36 Victor Serge, *Carnets (1936–1947)*, édition établie par Claudio Albertani et Claude Rioux (Marseille: Agone, 2012), 158.

37 Victor Serge, *Hitler contra Stalin, la fase decisiva de la guerra mundial*, traducción de Enrique Adroher (México, D.F.: Ediciones Quetzal, 1941).

38 See Richard Greeman, "Serge en México y México en Serge," in Victor Serge, *Los años sin perdón*, Alberto González Troyano, trans. (Xalapa, Mexico: Universidad Veracruzana, 2014).

39 Serge, *Memoirs*, 433.

40 Translated by Richard Greeman from "N.B. por Vlady," in *Mains/Manos: Un Poema de Victor Serge* (Mexico: Carta al Lector y El Taller Martín Pescador, 1978), a bilingual edition with a Spanish translation by Verónica Volkow.

ABOUT PM PRESS

PM Press was founded at the end of 2007 by a small collection of folks with decades of publishing, media, and organizing experience. PM Press co-conspirators have published and distributed hundreds of books, pamphlets, CDs, and DVDs. Members of PM have founded enduring book fairs, spearheaded victorious tenant organizing campaigns, and worked closely with bookstores, academic conferences, and even rock bands to deliver political and challenging ideas to all walks of life. We're old enough to know what we're doing and young enough to know what's at stake.

We seek to create radical and stimulating fiction and non-fiction books, pamphlets, T-shirts, visual and audio materials to entertain, educate, and inspire you. We aim to distribute these through every available channel with every available technology—whether that means you are seeing anarchist classics at our bookfair stalls, reading our latest vegan cookbook at the café, downloading geeky fiction e-books, or digging new music and timely videos from our website.

PM Press is always on the lookout for talented and skilled volunteers, artists, activists, and writers to work with. If you have a great idea for a project or can contribute in some way, please get in touch.

PM Press
PO Box 23912
Oakland, CA 94623
www.pmpress.org

FRIENDS OF PM PRESS

These are indisputably momentous times—the
financial system is melting down globally and
the Empire is stumbling. Now more than ever
there is a vital need for radical ideas.

In the years since its founding—and on a
mere shoestring—PM Press has risen to the formidable challenge
of publishing and distributing knowledge and entertainment for the
struggles ahead. With over 300 releases to date, we have published an
impressive and stimulating array of literature, art, music, politics, and
culture. Using every available medium, we've succeeded in connecting
those hungry for ideas and information to those putting them into
practice.

Friends of PM allows you to directly help impact, amplify, and revitalize
the discourse and actions of radical writers, filmmakers, and artists. It
provides us with a stable foundation from which we can build upon our
early successes and provides a much-needed subsidy for the materials
that can't necessarily pay their own way. You can help make that
happen—and receive every new title automatically delivered to your
door once a month—by joining as a Friend of PM Press. And, we'll throw
in a free T-shirt when you sign up.

Here are your options:

• **$30 a month** Get all books and pamphlets plus 50% discount on all
  webstore purchases

• **$40 a month** Get all PM Press releases (including CDs and DVDs)
  plus 50% discount on all webstore purchases

• **$100 a month** Superstar—Everything plus PM merchandise, free
  downloads, and 50% discount on all webstore purchases

For those who can't afford $30 or more a month, we're introducing
Sustainer Rates at $15, $10 and $5. Sustainers get a free PM Press
T-shirt and a 50% discount on all purchases from our website.

Your Visa or Mastercard will be billed once a month, until you tell us to
stop. Or until our efforts succeed in bringing the revolution around. Or
the financial meltdown of Capital makes plastic redundant. Whichever
comes first.

Men in Prison

Victor Serge
Introduction and Translation by
Richard Greeman

ISBN: 978-1-60486-736-7
$18.95   232 pages

"Everything in this book is fictional and
everything is true," wrote Victor Serge in the
epigraph to *Men in Prison*. "I have attempted,
through literary creation, to bring out the general meaning and human
content of a personal experience."

The author of *Men in Prison* served five years in French penitentiaries
(1912–1917) for the crime of "criminal association"—in fact for his
courageous refusal to testify against his old comrades, the infamous
"Tragic Bandits" of French anarchism. "While I was still in prison," Serge
later recalled, "fighting off tuberculosis, insanity, depression, the spiritual
poverty of the men, the brutality of the regulations, I already saw one
kind of justification of that infernal voyage in the possibility of describing
it. Among the thousands who suffer and are crushed in prison—and how
few men really know that prison!—I was perhaps the only one who could
try one day to tell all ... There is no novelist's hero in this novel, unless
that terrible machine, prison, is its real hero. It is not about 'me,' about a
few men, but about men, all men crushed in that dark corner of society."

Ironically, Serge returned to writing upon his release from a GPU prison
in Soviet Russia, where he was arrested as an anti-Stalinist subversive
in 1928. He completed *Men in Prison* (and two other novels) in "semi-
captivity" before he was rearrested and deported to the Gulag in 1933.
Serge's classic prison novel has been compared to Dostoyevsky's *House
of the Dead*, Koestler's *Spanish Testament*, Genet's *Miracle of the Rose*,
and Solzhenitsyn's *One Day in the Life of Ivan Denisovitch* both for its
authenticity and its artistic achievement.

This edition features a substantial new introduction by translator Richard
Greeman, situating the work in Serge's life and times.

"No purer book about the hell of prison has ever been written."
—Martin Seymour-Smith, *Scotsman*

*"There is nothing in any line or word of this fine novel which doesn't ring
true."*
—Publishers Weekly

Birth of Our Power

Victor Serge

ISBN: 978-1-62963-030-4
$18.95   256 pages

Birth of Our Power is an epic novel set in Spain, France, and Russia during the heady revolutionary years 1917–1919. Serge's tale begins in the spring of 1917, the third year of mass slaughter in the blood-and-rain-soaked trenches of World War I, when the flames of revolution suddenly erupt in Russia and Spain. Europe is "burning at both ends." Although the Spanish uprising eventually fizzles, in Russia the workers, peasants, and common soldiers are able to take power and hold it. Serge's "tale of two cities" is constructed from the opposition between Barcelona, the city "we" could not take, and Petrograd, the starving capital of the Russian Revolution, besieged by counter-revolutionary Whites. Between the romanticism of radicalized workers awakening to their own power in a sun-drenched Spanish metropolis to the grim reality of workers clinging to power in Russia's dark, frozen revolutionary outpost. From "victory-in-defeat" to "defeat in victory."

"*Nothing in it has dated… It is less an autobiography than a sustained, incandescent lyric (half-pantheist, half-surrealist) of rebellion and battle.*"
—*Times Literary Supplement*

"*Surely one of the most moving accounts of revolutionary experience ever written.*"
—Neal Ascherson, *New York Review of Books*

"*Probably the most remarkable of his novels… Of all the European writers who have taken revolution as their theme, Serge is second only to Conrad… Here is a writer with a magnificent eye for the panoramic sweep of historical events and an unsparingly precise moral insight.*"
—Francis King, *Sunday Telegraph*

"*Intense, vivid, glowing with energy and power… A wonderful picture of revolution and revolutionaries… The power of the novel is in its portrayal of the men who are involved.*"
—*Manchester Evening News*

"*Birth of Our Power is one of the finest romances of revolution ever written, and confirms Serge as an outstanding chronicler of his turbulent era… As an epic, Birth of Our Power has lost none of its strength.*"
—Lawrence M. Bensky, *New York Times*

Anarchists Never Surrender: Essays, Polemics, and Correspondence on Anarchism, 1908-1938

Victor Serge

ISBN: 978-1-62963-031-1
$20.00   256 pages

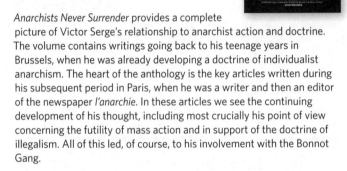

Anarchists Never Surrender provides a complete picture of Victor Serge's relationship to anarchist action and doctrine. The volume contains writings going back to his teenage years in Brussels, when he was already developing a doctrine of individualist anarchism. The heart of the anthology is the key articles written during his subsequent period in Paris, when he was a writer and then an editor of the newspaper *l'anarchie*. In these articles we see the continuing development of his thought, including most crucially his point of view concerning the futility of mass action and in support of the doctrine of illegalism. All of this led, of course, to his involvement with the Bonnot Gang.

His thought slowly but most definitely evolved during the period of his imprisonment for his association with Bonnot and his comrades. The anthology includes both his correspondence with his comrade Émile Armand and articles written immediately after his release from prison, among them the key letters that signify the beginning of his break with his individualist past and that point the way to his later engagement alongside the Bolsheviks. It also includes an essential article on Nietzschean thought. This collection also includes articles that Serge wrote after he had left anarchism behind, analyzing both the history and the state of anarchism and the ways in which he hoped anarchism would leaven the harshness and dictatorial tendencies of Bolshevism.

Anarchists Never Surrender anthologizes a variety of Serge texts nowhere previously available and fleshes out the portrait of this brilliant writer and thinker, who has reached new heights of popularity and interest.

"Serge is not merely a political writer; he is also a novelist, a wonderfully lyrical writer… He is a writer young rebels desperately need whether they know it or not… He does not tell us what we should feel; instead, he makes us feel it."
—Stanley Reynolds, *New Statesman*

"I can't think of anyone else who has written about the revolutionary movement in this century with Serge's combination of moral insight and intellectual richness."
—Dwight Macdonald

Everyone Has Their Reasons

Joseph Matthews

ISBN: 978-1-62963-094-6
$24.95   528 pages

On November 7, 1938, a small, slight seventeen-
year-old Polish-German Jew named Herschel
Grynszpan entered the German embassy in
Paris and shot dead a consular official. Three
days later, in supposed response, Jews across
Germany were beaten, imprisoned, and
killed, their homes, shops, and synagogues smashed and burned—
Kristallnacht, the Night of Broken Glass.

Based on the historical record and told through his "letters" from
German prisons, the novel begins in 1936, when fifteen-year-old
Herschel flees Germany. Penniless and alone, he makes it to Paris
where he lives hand-to-mouth, his shadow existence mixing him with
the starving and the wealthy, with hustlers, radicals, and seamy sides
of Paris nightlife. In 1938, the French state rejects refugee status for
Herschel and orders him out of the country. Soon after, the Nazis round
up all Polish Jews in Germany—including Herschel's family—and dump
them on the Poland border. Herschel's response is to shoot the German
official, then wait calmly for the French police. June 1940, Herschel
is still in prison awaiting trial when the Nazi army nears Paris. He is
evacuated but escapes and seeks protection at a prison in the far south
of France. Two weeks later the French state hands him to the Gestapo.
The Nazis plan a big show trial, inviting the world press to Berlin for the
spectacle, to demonstrate through Herschel that Jews had provoked
the war. Except that Herschel throws a last-minute wrench in the
plans, bringing the Nazi propaganda machine to a grinding halt. Hitler
himself postpones the trial and orders that no decision be made about
Herschel's fate until the Führer personally gives an order—one way or
another.

*"A tragic, gripping Orwellian tale of an orphan turned assassin in pre-World
War II Paris. Based on the true story of the Jewish teen Hitler blamed for
Kristallnacht, it's a wild ride through the underside of Europe as the storm
clouds of the Holocaust gather. Not to be missed!"*
—Terry Bisson, Hugo and Nebula award-winning author of *Fire on the
Mountain*

Voices of the Paris Commune

Edited by Mitchell Abidor

ISBN: 978-1-62963-100-4
$14.95   128 pages

The Paris Commune of 1871, the first instance of a working-class seizure of power, has been subject to countless interpretations; reviled by its enemies as a murderous bacchanalia of the unwashed while praised by supporters as an exemplar of proletarian anarchism in action. As both a successful model to be imitated and as a devastating failure to be avoided. All of the interpretations are tendentious. Historians view the working class's three-month rule through their own prism, distant in time and space. *Voices of the Paris Commune* takes a different tack. In this book only those who were present in the spring of 1871, who lived through and participated in the Commune, are heard.

The Paris Commune had a vibrant press, and it is represented here by its most important newspaper, *Le Cri du Peuple*, edited by Jules Vallès, member of the First International. Like any legitimate government, the Paris Commune held parliamentary sessions and issued daily printed reports of the heated, contentious deliberations that belie any accusation of dictatorship. Included in this collection is the transcript of the debate in the Commune, just days before its final defeat, on the establishing of a Committee of Public Safety and on the fate of the hostages held by the Commune, hostages who would ultimately be killed.

Finally, *Voices of the Paris Commune* contains a selection from the inquiry carried out twenty years after the event by the intellectual review *La Revue Blanche*, asking participants to judge the successes and failures of the Paris Commune. This section provides a fascinating range of opinions of this epochal event.

"The Paris Commune of 1871 has been the subject of much ideological debate, often far removed from the experiences of the participants themselves. If you really want to dig deep into what happened during those fateful weeks, reading these eyewitness accounts is mandatory."
—Gabriel Kuhn, editor of *All Power to the Councils! A Documentary History of the German Revolution of 1918–1919*

"The Paris Commune holds a place of pride in the hearts of radicals—heroically created from the bottom up and tragically crushed by the forces of reaction. Yet, as this collection illustrates, the lessons of the Commune, as debated by the Communards themselves, are as enduring and vital as that briefly liberated society was inspiring."
—Sasha Lilley, author of *Capital and Its Discontents*

Al-Mutanabbi Street Starts Here: Poets and Writers Respond to the March 5th, 2007, Bombing of Baghdad's "Street of the Booksellers"

Edited by Beau Beausoleil and Deema Shehabi

ISBN: 978-1-60486-590-5
$20.00   320 pages

On March 5th, 2007, a car bomb was exploded on al-Mutanabbi Street in Baghdad. More than thirty people were killed and more than one hundred were wounded. This locale is the historic center of Baghdad bookselling, a winding street filled with bookstores and outdoor book stalls. Named after the famed 10th century classical Arab poet al-Mutanabbi, it has been the heart and soul of the Baghdad literary and intellectual community. This anthology begins with a historical introduction to al-Mutanabbi Street and includes the writing of Iraqis as well as a wide swath of international poets and writers who were outraged by this attack.

This book seeks to show where al-Mutanabbi Street starts in all of us: personally, in our communities, and in our nations. It seeks to show the commonality between this small street in Baghdad and our own cultural centers, and why this attack was an attack on us all. This anthology sees al-Mutanabbi Street as a place for the free exchange of ideas; a place that has long offered its sanctuary to the complete spectrum of Iraqi voices. This is where the roots of democracy (in the best sense of that word) took hold many hundreds of years ago. This anthology looks toward al-Mutanabbi Street as an affirmation of all that we hope for in a more just society.

"This anthology celebrates the exquisite relationship between the book and the reader, humanity and culture, writing and life and love. It is a tribute to a street that grows into a large and archetypal symbol and spatial metaphor for books."
—Muhsin al-Musawi, professor of Arabic and Comparative Studies at Columbia University and editor of the *Journal of Arabic Literature*

"The collection of materials in this anthology is astounding and harrowing. Beausoleil and Shehabi have put together a book that will be adored by lovers of poetry, essays, journalism, and testimony. It will also be required reading for anyone interested in social justice."
—Steven Salaita, associate professor of English, Virginia Tech University

A Declaration of the Rights of Human Beings: On the Sovereignty of Life as Surpassing the Rights of Man, Second Edition

Raoul Vaneigem

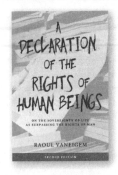

ISBN: 978-1-62963-155-4
$20.00   192 pages

"A declaration of rights is indispensable in order to halt the ravages of despotism." So wrote the revolutionary Antoine Barnave in support of the Declaration of the Rights of Man and of the Citizen (1789). Over two centuries after the Great French Revolution, Raoul Vaneigem writes that today, "in a situation comparable to the condition of France on the eve of its Revolution," we cannot limit ourselves to demanding liberties—the so-called bourgeois freedoms—that came into being with free trade, for now the free exchange of capital is the totalitarian form of a system which reduces human beings and the earth itself to merchandise. The time has come to give priority to the real individual rather than to Man in the abstract, the citizen answerable to the State and to the sole dictates of God's successor, the Economy.

Sometimes playful or poetic, always provocative, Raoul Vaneigem reviews the history of bills of rights before offering his own call, with commentary, for fifty-seven rights yet to be won in a world where the "freedoms accorded to Man" are no longer merely "the freedoms accorded by man to the economy." Every human being has the right, for example: to become human and to be treated as such; to dispose freely of his or her time; to comfort and luxury; to free modes of transport set up by and for the collectivity; to permanent control over scientific experimentation; to association by affinity; to reconciliation with his or her animal nature; to bend toward life what was turned toward death; to the flux of passions and the freedoms of love; to a natural life and a natural death; to stray, to get lost and find him or herself; to hold nothing sacred; to excess and to moderation; to desire what seems beyond the realm of the possible.

Readers of Vaneigem's now-classic work *The Revolution of Everyday Life*, which as one of the main contributions of the Situationist International was a harbinger of May 1968 in France, will find much to savor in these pages written in the highest idiom of subversive utopianism.

"All opponents of globalization should carry it in their luggage."
—*Le Monde*

The Revolution of Everyday Life

Raoul Vaneigem

Translated by Donald Nicholson-Smith

ISBN: 978-1-60486-678-0
$20.00   288 pages

Originally published just months before
the May 1968 upheavals in France, Raoul
Vaneigem's *The Revolution of Everyday Life*
offered a lyrical and aphoristic critique of the "society of the spectacle"
from the point of view of individual experience. Whereas Debord's
masterful analysis of the new historical conditions that triggered the
uprisings of the 1960s armed the revolutionaries of the time with theory,
Vaneigem's book described their feelings of desperation directly, and
armed them with "formulations capable of firing point-blank on our
enemies."

"I realise," writes Vaneigem in his introduction, "that I have given
subjective will an easy time in this book, but let no one reproach me
for this without first considering the extent to which the objective
conditions of the contemporary world advance the cause of subjectivity
day after day."

Vaneigem names and defines the alienating features of everyday life
in consumer society: survival rather than life, the call to sacrifice, the
cultivation of false needs, the dictatorship of the commodity, subjection
to social roles, and above all the replacement of God by the Economy.
And in the second part of his book, "Reversal of Perspective," he explores
the countervailing impulses that, in true dialectical fashion, persist
within the deepest alienation: creativity, spontaneity, poetry, and the
path from isolation to communication and participation.

For "To desire a different life is already that life in the making." And
"fulfillment is expressed in the singular but conjugated in the plural."

The present English translation was first published by Rebel Press of
London in 1983. This new edition of *The Revolution of Everyday Life* has
been reviewed and corrected by the translator and contains a new
preface addressed to English-language readers by Raoul Vaneigem. The
book is the first of several translations of works by Vaneigem that PM
Press plans to publish in uniform volumes. Vaneigem's classic work is to
be followed by *The Knight, the Lady, the Devil, and Death* (2003) and *The
Inhumanity of Religion* (2000).